GOOD TAKEOFFS
AND
GOOD LANDINGS

JOE CHRISTY

GOOD TAKEOFFS
AND
GOOD LANDINGS

JOE CHRISTY

TAB BOOKS Inc.

Blue Ridge Summit, PA

FIRST EDITION
FIRST PRINTING

Copyright © 1988 by TAB BOOKS Inc.
Printed in the United States of America

Library of Congress Cataloging in Publication Data

Christy, Joe.
Good takeoffs and good landings / by Joe Christy.
p.   cm.
Includes index.
ISBN 0-8306-0387-5   ISBN 0-8306-0287-9 (pbk.)
1. Airplanes—Landing.   I. Title.
TL711.L3C48   1987
629.132′5213—dc19   87-29045
                                          CIP

Questions regarding the content of this book
should be addressed to:

Reader Inquiry Branch
TAB BOOKS Inc.
Blue Ridge Summit, PA 17294-0214

Contents

Introduction

IF THERE IS A SINGLE PREREQUISITE FOR MAKING CONSISTENTLY GOOD takeoffs and landings, it is that you have to work at it—new student pilot or 10,000-hour veteran, you have to work at it. It never gets any easier; it just seems easier to those who develop good techniques and to whom precision becomes a habit.

The problem is, there is no single procedure that is effective in all conditions, and the last thing a student or low-time pilot wants to hear is that "it takes experience." Experience is a tardy teacher.

There are stylized procedures that will ensure safe and acceptable takeoffs and landings under most conditions. These are what you learn by rote—the things you can do by the numbers. Add some common sense, along with a thorough understanding of the aerodynamic forces involved, and you can—with effort and concentration—ad-lib the fine tuning required to make enviable takeoffs and landings.

The "aerodynamic forces involved" are, of course, the true keys, and we will make a detailed investigation of them with regard to control-handling techniques and your assessment of each takeoff and landing situation.

Included are the common transitional operations attendant to takeoffs and landings, as well as radio communication procedures, because all have a bearing—either directly or indirectly—upon the planning and execution of these actions.

This book is intended as a practical, hands-on guide for beginning and low-time pilots. I've avoided theory and mathematical formulas in favor of straightforward, useful data and advice.

1

The Basics

OVER THE YEARS, MUCH HAS BEEN SAID ABOUT THE "TRUE" FUNCTIONS of an airplane's flight controls. I know an instructor who tells his students that the rudder should be regarded as a "trimming device." My instructor, back in the 1930s, was fond of saying that you should think of the throttle as the "up-and-down" control, and some instructors insist that, in or near a stall, wings must be leveled with rudder, never aileron.

There is nothing wrong with any of the above, although each could stand some elaboration. There are a lot of "howevers" in flying, and it's necessary to qualify just about everything you say about the action and effect of the flight controls. For example, many instructors like to say that "pitch plus power equals performance." That, too, is correct, but it doesn't say where the power comes from. With no thrust from your engine, you glide using gravity for power—if you have previously stored sufficient energy in the form of altitude.

Saying it that way, we stumble onto one of the secrets of safe flight— *stored energy*. As long as you have excess speed or altitude to spend, you have a margin of safety, and these two forms of energy are almost always interchangeable. That is what makes it possible to teach that there are times when the control wheel controls altitude (an instrument approach, for example), and times when the control wheel controls airspeed (during climbout following takeoff, for example).

Actually, it's all in the way you think about it. During climbout, you are controlling the rate of climb by referencing the airspeed. If you had an angle-of-attack indicator, it would serve the same purpose (if your owner's manual classified climbs that way), because that is what you are actually controlling with the forward and backward movement of the control wheel.

Angle of Attack

The whole story of controlled flight is contained in a single term: *angle of attack*. Everything an airplane does in flight depends upon the angle at which its wing meets the supporting sea of air. If air were visible, flying would be easier, because we could see what was happening as the air flowed over and around our wings. But because it is not, we avoid talking about angles of attack as much as possible, and refer instead to the "pitch" attitude of our aircraft (Fig. 1-1); the nose is pitched up and pitched down—despite the fact that "up" and "down" are not always up and down in relation to the direction you want the nose to go. It's better to say that up-elevator (back pressure on the control wheel) pulls the nose toward the pilot, while down-elevator (forward pressure on the control wheel) pushes the nose away from the pilot—or, back pressure increases angle of attack, and forward pressure decreases angle of attack. *These statements are true regardless of your airplane's attitude in relation to the ground.*

Angle of attack is more precisely defined as the angle between the *chord line* of the wing (a straight line from the foremost point of the leading edge to the trailing edge) and the *relative wind*. Relative wind results from the movement of your aircraft through the air. It is the airflow over an airfoil, and is parallel to and in the opposite direction of the flight path of the airplane (Fig. 1-2).

Maximum angle of attack is between 15° and 18°, no matter what your airspeed, attitude, or other flight condition. Tip the wing up at an angle greater than this critical angle, and the smooth airflow around the wing—especially over its upper surfaces, which provide most of the lift—is broken up and the wing stalls.

Normally, you have no reason to exceed an angle of attack greater than about 10°. Your best *rate* of climb will be less than that, and although best *angle* of climb can be as much as 15° (and therefore nibbling at the edge of a stall), it is not exactly a normal maneuver. In any case, these figures are not very useful in the real world, because no one can accurately eyeball such measurements, especially when the wings are not level. True, the artificial horizon will show a 10-degree climb, but that indicates where the nose is pointing—not necessarily with respect to the relative wind.

Fig. 1-1. The airplane's three axes are shown on this photo of Beechcraft Musketeer Eight Four Juliet. Pitch is controlled by the elevators (or stabilator in this case), yaw is controlled by the rudder, and roll (bank) is controlled by the ailerons—well, primarily. There are a lot of "howevers" in flying.

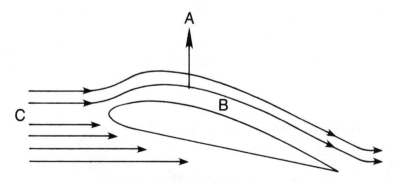

Fig. 1-2. The relative wind results from the movement of an aircraft through the air (C). The low pressure area (B) is created by the wing's shape. The center of lift (A) moves forward as the angle of attack increases. At extreme angles of attack, the airflow over the wing's upper surface begins to burble at the trailing edge and moves forward, following the center of lift until lift is destroyed, unless angle of attack is reduced.

So, it would seem that we are not gaining much on this subject. We have knowledge that is of questionable value to us when we're in the airplane, turning final, watching for other traffic, and trying to keep the airspeed nailed. What we need are concepts that always promote proper control techniques. We can't trust our nervous system just because it has memorized the feel of the airplane. It is easily confused and is responsible for the crossed controls that result in the many stall-spin fatalities in airport traffic patterns every year. In other words, we are not going to achieve maximum safety and precision with seat-of-the-pants reactions.

What about those concepts, and why have we labored through all this angle-of-attack stuff if it is not useful in the real world of flying? Well, if we had angle-of-attack indicators in our airplanes (modern jet fighters have them), that would certainly aid precision and safety. And our ultimate concepts are going to be based on angle of attack even if we don't use that term. That's why.

Orville and Wilbur are said to have had an angle-of-attack indicator—a piece of string attached to the front of their machine. Actually, that would be a relative wind indicator. It would be a helpful device, if the loose end didn't whip around so much (I had one during my brief ultralight experience), although you would have to add the wings' *angle of incidence* to the estimated angle of attack indicated by the string in order to get total angle of attack.

The angle of incidence can be described as "built-in" angle of attack. It results from the fact that wings are attached to the fuselage with their leading edges tipped upward 1–3° so that there is a positive angle of attack in level flight. (The B-52 bomber has an incidence angle so great that the aircraft seems to levitate, rather than rotate, on takeoff—it goes up with the fuselage apparently level).

An angle-of-attack indicator has long been available for light aircraft, but pilots have never lined up to buy it. Perhaps that is because our instructors conditioned us to think of pitch rather than angle of attack, and because we have stall-warning devices in the cockpit which begin to complain about the way we are mishandling the airplane *before* our wings reach their critical angle of attack.

Human nature being as it is, some of us acquire the habit of discounting the urgent message of the stall-warning horn. These pilots glance at the airspeed and tell themselves that they have a few knots to play with before reaching the actual stall. I've ridden with pilots who had their stall warners sounding yards before reaching the threshold of an 8,000-foot runway, and with the Visual Approach Slope Indicators (VASI) on the ground all red. The only thing that saves such an approach is a judicious use of power.

Flying in visual meteorological conditions, we judge the safe angle-of-attack range primarily by reference to external indicators—aircraft nose and wingtips in relation to the horizon—backed up by a check of the attitude indicator and perhaps the airspeed indicator. The vertical-speed indicator (VSI) tells us a little something about angle of attack only indirectly, and has a significant lag to boot. The attitude indicator (artificial horizon) provides instant information, and you can easily determine a 10-degree positive angle of attack from it when the wings are fairly level (with a little effort, perhaps, in turning flight). Ten degrees, plus your built-in angle of incidence (which can be as much as 3°), begins to crowd your maximum allowable angle of attack.

So, it isn't too hard to visualize your angle of attack in level flight. It's when you start to turn that your angle-of-attack indicators—both outside and in the cockpit—become fuzzy.

You do have other indicators. One of them is G-load. My instructor back in the stone age of flight had a favorite saying: "Keep the load off yourself and you won't overload the airplane."

He was talking about G-load, of course, and his idea of an acceptable G-load ranged between the approximately 1.2 G's of a 30-degree banked turn, and the 1.4 G's of a 45-degree banked turn. He frowned on turns banked beyond 45°, but liked to demonstrate them at 60° and tell his students that they, and the airplane, possessed twice their normal weight in such a turn—which was, of course, self-evident (Fig. 1-3).

He even had a "strain gauge" for the wings that was a most effective device for convincing students that excessive back pressure on the control stick was to be avoided lest the wings suddenly depart the aircraft. The strain gauge was a length of soft baling wire that ran from the point between the wings of the Spartan biplane where the flying and landing wires crossed, to the engine mount. Normally, the wire was loose, and I never

Fig. 1-3. Keep the load off yourself and you'll never overload the airplane's structure. The higher the airspeed when an airplane is stalled, the higher the load factor.

was sure whether my instructor actually knew how much of a G-load was required to make the wire tight. He claimed that the wings had to bend backwards four inches to tighten the strain gauge. I'm not sure that I believed that. But if you ever saw that bit of wire vibrating taut as a bow string, I doubt you'd ever forget it. I never have.

Another indication that angle of attack is significantly increasing and airspeed is decreasing, is a loosening-up of the controls, a situation that you should recognize from your slow-flight practice during your initial instruction. Perhaps your instructor mentioned that slow flight equates with increased angles of attack. You probably noticed that, in slow flight, the nose rode a little higher in relation to the horizon.

The airspeed indicator is an indirect source of angle-of-attack information. In turning flight, it is second only to the attitude indicator for such reference. You can, of course, temporarily exceed the wings' critical angle of attack at *any* airspeed with abrupt and excessive back pressure on the control yoke, but operating in normal flight regimes, applying normal control pressures, you can rely on the airspeed indicator to provide information relative to the stall.

The Four Basic Flight Conditions

Your instructor will tell you, the better how-to-fly books will tell you, and I will tell you: You cannot hope to become a truly competent pilot until you have mastered the four basic flight conditions—straight-and-level, climbs, turns, and descents. All flight maneuvers involve one or more of these conditions, including takeoffs and landings. You will not be able to consistently perform good takeoffs and landings until the four fundamentals are consistently flown with a high degree of precision.

It's not easy. The books that tell you how easy it is to learn to fly were written to sell, not to use. Sure, after 10 or 12 hours of dual almost anyone can take off, smoke around the pattern, and get the airplane back on the ground right side up. To those who decide that is good enough, one of two things will eventually happen: they will kill themselves (and probably several others, as well), in an airplane or they will luck-out of a situation that frightens them to the edge of panic and then decide to quit flying. Rarely do incompetent pilots decide to expend the effort necessary to become safe and competent ones. Had they possessed the "right stuff," they would have established a higher goal in the first place.

So, I recommend that you be honest with yourself about your goals as a pilot. If you have a track record of not finishing things you start, if you habitually seek the easiest way to do things, and if you regularly spend more than you earn, the sensible course is to forget flying and instead take up an activity that is less exacting in its demands on you.

Straight and Level

Most flight instructors will begin your flight training with straight-and-level practice. Some students are impatient with such a prosaic approach to learning to fly, but that is where precision begins, and the ability to hold a heading within 10° will determine your score on the FAA private flight test (5° on more advanced tests). You'll have to be even more precise during instrument landing approaches.

The ability to hold a constant altitude, with wings level, is the rest of the equation. It takes practice, and the mental practice is as important as the physical practice. You are not only imposing upon your nervous system the countless tiny corrections necessary for good straight-and-level, but you are also impressing the *habit* of precision upon your mind (Fig. 1-4).

Fig. 1-4. Straight-and-level is where precision begins and both inside and outside references are established.

The proliferation of affordable autopilots in lightplanes tends to erode pilot proficiency in straight-and-level flight because the autopilot will fly the airplane in cross-country cruise with great precision while significantly decreasing pilot fatigue. If your airplane is so equipped, you should periodically give "George" a rest and hand-fly your machine.

In VFR conditions, your straight-and-level indicators are primarily outside the airplane—the position of the engine cowling and wingtips in relation to the horizon—backed up by a quick scan of two or three flight instruments. Actually, a glance at the attitude indicator should be sufficient, because it indicates both pitch and bank.

Several flight instruments report changes in attitude. The VSI, the altimeter, and the airspeed indicator will all gain or lose with changes in pitch and no compensating change in power. If you have no directional gyro, the turn coordinator is hard to beat for detecting heading changes as they occur in this kind of practice. Navigating cross-country, you'll be using your VOR course deviation needle or magnetic compass.

Once you are stabilized on what you believe to be straight-and-level (we'll discuss transitions to straight-and-level from climbs and descents momentarily) with the desired power, mixture, and RPM settings, check the attitude indicator and VSI to confirm zero pitch, then return your attention to external references.

Observe where the wingtips ride in relation to the horizon. When viewed from between the two front seats, both left and right tips will be the same distance above (for high-wings) or below (for low-wings) that reference. Note, too, the amount that the leading edges are tipped upward. Then snap a mental picture of how the top of the engine cowling appears in relation to the horizon ahead. In most lightplanes, the top of the cowling, depending upon where along its sloping surface your line of sight is fixed, will be several inches below the horizon. You will quickly establish your own mental images of the external straight-and-level indicators for each airplane you fly.

The Stylized Scan

The need to remain vigilant for other air traffic and to learn to divide your attention between the outside and inside of your aircraft argues for the development of a scanning habit that (1) provides an ongoing visual check of the sky around you, (2) includes the external straight-and-level references, and (3) instills an "instrument awareness" factor in your mind. It is a simple concept and one that is easy to initiate.

You may start anywhere and vary the sequence to suit yourself. The important thing is to develop a stylized scan habit so that you will do it without conscious thought. You can begin by looking as far behind the left wing as possible without straining. Then, at a measured pace—not slow, not fast—turn your head to allow your gaze to sweep from left to right outside the airplane, noting your cowl/horizon reference (and a distant landmark if you are using such to maintain your track by pilotage). Continue the scan as far to the right as you can comfortably see. Anytime you have a passenger in the right seat, put him or her to work watching for traffic on the right. On the return sweep, include the instrument panel.

If you are familiar with the airplane it isn't necessary to actually *read* instruments and gauges most of the time. You will know where the needles should be pointing, and any that are out of place will stand out. The frequency of your scan is up to you, and may be influenced by weather, type and density of traffic, visibility, and the kind of airplane you are flying.

Your scan can be a very effective safety procedure in the airport traffic pattern. Because your attention must constantly be divided between inside and outside indicators in the pattern, you undoubtedly will abbreviate your scan somewhat, but you must not ignore the instrument panel.

Turns

Most accidents in airport traffic patterns occur during turns—turns from the downwind to base leg, and from base to final approach (Fig. 1-5). The accidents happen as the result of a stalled condition, usually with crossed controls—in other words, in steep turns. If we stop and consider all the things that are against us in steep turns (more than, say, 35° of bank), most of us would avoid them like the plague: (1) the steeper the turn, the more you give up in the way of external references that aid in maintaining level flight, (2) the airspeed indicator is subject to error, (3) the G-load causes an increase in stall speed, and (4) you are led into a crossed-control situation that, after about 40–45° of bank, seems to indicate that nothing is working the way it should. The airplane has a marked tendency to increase the bank angle, and you must hold opposite aileron against that force. Meanwhile, you feel the need to feed-in more and more rudder (in the direction of the turn) to maintain a constant turn rate, while increasing the back pressure on the control yoke to "pull" the airplane around the turn. With the horizon ahead tilted at 45° or more, it is no longer very useful as a pitch reference. The stall warner sounds and, if you have time (remember, you are 800–1,000 feet AGL), your next inclination is to check the airspeed indicator, but that reading doesn't seem to make sense. The relative wind is entering the pitot head at an angle, and perhaps buffeting the static port as well. Without quick and

Fig. 1-5. Keep your turns shallow in the traffic pattern. If a steep turn is needed to correct for poor timing, it is usually safer to "go around."

proper action at this point, most airplanes will stall, whip inverted, and dive into the ground. This happens a predictable number of times each year.

Sure, it's depressing. But reduced-speed turns at low altitude are part of every airport traffic pattern. There is no way you can avoid performing them. But you *can* master them.

You know how to make normal turns, banked 30° or less, and as a private pilot you could fly for years without exceeding 35° of bank. The secret is good planning. No matter how much it hurts, you've got to *think* in an airplane.

Practicing turns, you should turn a predetermined amount—say, 90°. (I don't mean a bank angle of 90°!) Then practice turns of 45°, 180°, and 360°. If you do your 360s properly you may feel the bump of your own propwash as you return to your original heading. You should practice turns referenced to an external landmark and ones referenced to your directional gyro. They are not the same.

Some pilots believe that the turn coordinator, which has largely replaced the old needle-and-ball instrument, indicates angle of bank. It does not. What it tells you is direction and *rate* of turn. The little airplane merely replaced the gyro-controlled needle of the earlier instrument. And many pilots have been taught to "step on the ball" when it moves from its cage. Actually, you can cage the ball two ways: If the ball sinks to the inside of your turn, you can add rudder or reduce bank; if the ball rises to the outside of your turn, you can reduce rudder or add bank.

But I maintain that stepping on the ball is inefficient, and in heavy aircraft—that is, heavier than a training airplane—it is dangerous at low airspeeds. Some years ago, the Army taught it one way, the Navy another. A friend who is a pilot instructor in Air Force C-5As says he was taught that ailerons control the ball and rudder controls the needle.

Clearly, it is taught both ways, but I believe one way is more consistent with the entire range of flight maneuvers, and is certainly more consistent with safe operating practices at low airspeeds. If you have been taught to "step on the ball" to cage it, ask your instructor about this. One thing you can almost always count on from a CFI is a good and sincere response to the student pilot who displays an honest desire to work and learn.

Where's the Wind?

Another of the basics which sometimes causes confusion has to do with the effects of wind on the forces which sustain your airplane in flight—perhaps instead of "wind" I should say "the direction of movement of the air mass through which you are flying." You must fully understand your relationship with the wind when airborne. If you do, you aren't likely to be trapped into the ancient "downwind turn" controversy in the pilots' lounge (Fig. 1-6). I have a friend who writes about flying and who has been a pilot for more than 25 years. He always adds a touch of power when making a downwind turn in the lower altitudes. It doesn't do any harm, and I long ago gave up trying to convince him that there is no difference between downwind, upwind, or crosswind turns in flight. They are all the same to the airplane. You will lose a little airspeed during *any* level turn—not because of any wind effect, but because part of your total energy is diverted to lift the airplane around the turn. Vertical lift no longer offsets gravity when a bank is established, because the wings' lift (i.e., the total lift) is at an angle to gravity's pull. Some back pressure on the yoke increases angle of attack and compensates for the loss of vertical lift. But without an increase in power, the price paid is a slight drop in airspeed during the turn, regardless of wind direction.

I once heard an experienced agricultural pilot say that he could feel the difference between downwind and upwind turns. Close to the surface,

Fig. 1-6. To an airplane in flight, there is no difference between downwind, crosswind, or upwind turns except when flying through a wind shear.

the difference is certainly evident in the ground track, but it is nothing that the airplane can feel. The 90-degree turn from a downwind to a crosswind track requires *more* than a 90-degree heading change. The drift is going to be quite evident close to the ground. You will turn *less* than 90° to achieve a 90-degree change in ground track when turning from upwind to crosswind. Remember, when airborne, you are carried *with* a moving air mass independently of your movement *through* it. The ground track maneuvers practiced as a student pilot are supposed to give you an understanding of this relationship.

Entering a turn, coordinate yoke and rudder. The exact amount of rudder required for a given bank angle is one of those things you learn by doing. In medium-banked turns in most lightplanes, you will return the controls to neutral after the turn is established. In shallow turns, you will have to hold some control pressures into the turn because the dihedral (the angle at which the wings are joined to the fuselage) tends to return the aircraft to level flight. In steep turns, you will find yourself holding opposite aileron to counter the airplane's overbanking tendency after you exceed about 45° of bank. No single set of instructions covers control techniques in all kinds of turns.

You will lead your recovery from a turn by an amount commensurate with the turn rate. I wish I could think of a way to say that more precisely, but again, this is one of the things you'll have to learn by doing. The feel of the airplane controls, like the feel of your automobile's controls, is memorized by your nervous system and soon becomes automatic. In controlling an airplane, however, you have to consider a third dimension, and you can't trust your nervous system when it is denied input from your eyes.

When you bank the airplane, the down aileron adds both lift and drag on its side. That wing rises, but also momentarily slows, which causes the nose to yaw towards the up wing. That is why, to make a balanced turn, you need to feed-in rudder in the direction of the turn. Too much rudder and you'll skid the turn, while too little rudder will allow the airplane to slip toward the inside of the turn.

Another force is involved here—that of the propeller. I will get to it momentarily because it is to be reckoned within takeoff and climb as well.

Earlier, I mentioned "stored energy" and the fact that altitude, range, and airspeed are on deposit in the same account. To a limited extent, all are interchangeable; spend one and you are left with more of the others.

In an earlier book, discussing this subject, I suggested a simple demonstration that I picked up from an instructor friend: You are trimmed for straight-and-level flight, cruising at 65-percent power. Now, without moving any other controls, advance the throttle. Do you speed up? No. You begin to climb.

You were straight-and-level, and you didn't pull back the wheel to raise the nose. Why didn't you simply gain airspeed?

Well, additional power meant more lift at that angle of attack. Had you wanted to increase airspeed, it would have been necessary to decrease your angle of attack when you added more power. You see, straight-and-level, using 65-percent of your available power, you had the airplane trimmed to whatever angle of attack was required to exactly balance lift against gravity. Additional power meant added lift. You could have remained straight-and-level, while increasing airspeed, with forward pressure on the control wheel, and then retrimming to fly at the decreased angle of attack.

You could have climbed by applying back pressure on the control wheel (for awhile, at least), in which case you would have done so at the expense of airspeed (Fig. 1-7). Such a trade-off is limited because it requires that you have excess airspeed (thrust) to be traded. Back pressure on the control wheel increases the angle of attack, and that demands additional thrust—thrust which must be subtracted from the straight-and-level thrust.

In practice, you will normally make minor altitude corrections with pitch—with back pressure or forward pressure on the control wheel—because the airspeed changes are relatively insignificant. And learning to fly instruments, you will be told to control altitude with pitch and airspeed with power. On instruments, power and pitch adjustments are small, however, and your throttle remains your primary up-and-down control. As I said, there are a lot of "howevers" in flying.

Fig. 1-7. Back pressure on the yoke in cruising flight will give you a momentary climb at the expense of airspeed. Think of your engine as your primary climb control.

Torque and P-Factor

In the process of converting the engine's power into usable thrust, the propeller creates *torque*, and when the airplane is in any attitude except straight-and-level, the propeller is also responsible for a force known as *P-factor*.

Propeller torque is an example of Newton's Third Law of Motion, which holds that for every action there is an equal and opposite reaction. The crankshafts—and therefore the propellers—of aircraft piston engines manufactured in the U.S. rotate clockwise as viewed by the pilot (assuming that the engine is on the front of the airplane). The "equal and opposite reaction" to the propeller's clockwise rotation is a twisting force in the opposite direction (counterclockwise) exerted on the engine and airframe. Because the airplane's mass far exceeds that of the propeller, this part of the propeller's "side effects" is relatively insignificant in lightplanes. It is, however, reinforced by the effect of *spiraling propwash* ("propwash" is an ancient term that describes the disturbed air sent back by the propeller). As air is dragged through the rotating propeller blades, it is thrust rearward in a spiraling motion. This twisting column of air strikes the *left* side of the fuselage and vertical stabilizer to produce a yawing force to the left. The combined effects of propeller torque and spiraling propwash require some right rudder for correction at airspeeds below normal cruise. The airplane is rigged, usually with an offset vertical stabilizer or engine mounting, to compensate for propeller torque at normal cruising airspeeds.

P-factor, which becomes evident at low airspeeds with high RPM and high angles of attack, as in a climb, is owed to the fact that the descending propeller blade (on the right side as viewed by the pilot) meets the oncoming air at a greater angle of attack than the ascending blade. So more thrust is generated on the right side in the nose-up attitude. This, too, contributes to a left-turning tendency, and is yet another reason that right rudder is needed during takeoff and climb.

Climbs

In VFR operation, climbs should be performed using flight instruments and outside visual references. Shallow S-turns during climb help clear your forward blind spots and also make you more visible to other air traffic.

Any kind of climbing turn takes practice because, if you are to maintain a constant turn rate and bank angle, you must have good coordination in pitch, roll, and yaw simultaneously. You cannot expect to hold a constant airspeed and pitch attitude because you must pay for the turn with lift and airspeed.

Straight climbs are fairly simple in training airplanes. You usually climb at full throttle, adjust airspeed with pitch to hold V_y (best climb rate) or slightly faster as instructed by the owner's manual, and trim away control-wheel back pressure. Due to torque effect and P-factor, a little right rudder is necessary to counter the left-turning tendency. Because the nose of the airplane obscures the ground directly ahead, you reference the directional gyro to maintain a straight track. The wingtips can be useful in helping you to maintain a straight track if there is a highway, railroad, or some other prominent surface feature some distance away but parallel to your track.

In high-performance lightplanes, you have additional considerations. If the engine has a takeoff power rating and a maximum continuous rating, you must reduce power shortly after takeoff. Most pilots reduce power after takeoff even when there is no requirement to do so. With most engines, there's no reason why you can't climb at full power as long as the engine gauges remain in their green ranges.

Equipped with a constant-speed propeller, when reducing power after takeoff, back off the throttle (manifold pressure) first and then the propeller control (RPM), except on geared Lycomings. Normally aspirated engines will lose about 1″ Hg per 1,000 feet of altitude during climb.

Some lightplane pilots, flying the simpler machines, do not bother the mixture control until leveling off for cruising flight (especially if climbing at full throttle), under the assumption that the rich mixture is helping to cool the cylinder heads and exhaust valves. If you select a prolonged cruise-climb to get across country faster, you might want to lean the mixture to about 150° on the rich side of peak EGT, and remember that your cowl flaps are your primary means of regulating cylinder head temperature (CHT), which should not exceed 450° F.

With the smaller engines, equipped with fixed-pitch props, the time-honored procedure is to lean until the engine begins to run a little rough and then enrichen the mixture enough to smooth it out. Monitor the oil temperature if it is the only engine heat gauge you have, and further enrich the mixture as necessary. The main reason that air-cooled engines get poorer fuel economy than liquid-cooled engines is because air-cooled engines require richer fuel mixtures to hold down cylinder head and exhaust-valve/valve-guide temperatures.

To establish cruising flight at the end of your climbout following take-off, anticipate leveling off before reaching your desired altitude. Start to level off approximately 50 feet below your selected cruise altitude. Lower the nose gradually, and re-trim the airplane. You will lose altitude if you lower the nose to level flight without allowing the airspeed to build proportionately.

To accelerate to the desired cruising speed, temporarily maintain climb power after the airplane is in a level attitude. When you reach your desired cruising airspeed, or slightly above it, back off the throttle to the cruise power you have selected, adjust the mixture control, and re-trim. If your aircraft is equipped with a constant-speed propeller, when reducing power always retard the throttle first, then the RPM; when increasing power, always adjust the RPM first, then advance the throttle.

There is no precise correlation between manifold pressure and RPM. Any combination is acceptable as long as it produces the desired result and the associated engine gauges behave. During World War II, Charles Lindbergh went to the Pacific to show P-38 pilots how to greatly increase the range of their aircraft with high manifold pressure and low RPM settings.

Glides and Descents

You can intentionally descend with partial power or no power. With power off you adjust the pitch attitude to maintain airspeed and accept whatever rate of descent results. With partial power, use the amount of power needed to obtain your desired airspeed, while controlling the rate of descent with pitch attitude.

To initiate a power-off descent, first apply carburetor heat about one minute before starting the descent, and then back off the throttle. Never "chop" the throttle. There is no normal situation in which the throttle should be operated abruptly.

Reduced torque will require some corrective left rudder. Hold the nose level until the airspeed drops to near the normal descent airspeed, then lower the nose and establish the proper airspeed with the control wheel. Trim away the control-wheel pressure. The descent airspeed with power off is usually about 1.3 times the stall speed, and close to the airplane's best rate-of-climb airspeed.

Once your descent is stabilized, you will be wise to make shallow S-turns in order to clear the blind spot below your airplane's nose and reduce the possibility of letting down into other traffic. The habit of making clearing or S-turns during climbs and descents is about as prevalent as thorough preflight inspections, and the worst offenders are the guys with fat logbooks and macho images of themselves. Their unspoken message to other pilots, especially to student pilots, is: "Hey, boy, I've been flying so long that the rules don't apply to me. All that safety jazz is for the inexperienced."

Be advised, my fellow aeronauts, thorough preflights are for everyone. I recall the takeoff crash of an airplane that was not preflighted. A pencil was found jammed in the elevator hinge. Fuel exhaustion (due to a variety of causes, from mud daubers in fuel tank vents to faulty gauges) is another more common danger that is sometimes averted by the preflight inspection.

So much for the lecture; now back to descents. A partial-power descent is entered the same as a power-off descent. As you slow to the desired airspeed, lower the nose to the pitch attitude that produces the desired rate of descent as revealed by the VSI, adjust power to maintain the desired airspeed, and then trim away the elevator pressure.

Both types of let-downs are terminated the same way. Lead the recovery as you do when leveling off from a climb; otherwise, your inertia will carry you below your intended altitude. Smoothly add power as you raise the nose to a level attitude, and then re-trim. Return the carburetor-heat knob to the "cold" position.

Shock Cooling

Not long ago, a highly experienced aircraft mechanic told me he'd wager that at least half of all the engines in civilian training planes have cracked cylinder heads. When I asked him what prompted such a statement, he explained that trainers, such as the Cessna 150/152, are more subject to shock cooling than other lightplanes. He added the unsettling statement that too many young flight instructors today are careless about teaching students proper engine operating procedures, and this lack of knowledge is carried over into the student's future flying in larger aircraft, resulting in expensive damage to those engines.

Monitoring engine gauges and keeping those needles corralled in safe operating ranges is not enough. Rough handling of the throttle can damage an engine, as can *shock cooling*. Shock cooling to an air-cooled airplane engine occurs when the engine is allowed (or forced) to cool too rapidly, usually during letdown following extended cruise. In operation, all parts of the engine are not the same temperature. The cylinder heads, exhaust valves, and valve guides function at much higher temperatures than the rest of the engine and are the components most at risk if the engine cools too quickly.

The hairline cracks that can result from shock cooling of the cylinder heads are most common around the exhaust valve seats and radiating from spark plug holes. The valves can stick and warp, and the exhaust valve seats can become deformed. One common result is bent push rods caused by sticking valves. All of this argues in favor of partial-power descents to prevent shock cooling.

The need to develop a smooth, unhurried touch on the throttle will be magnified anytime you are flying an engine that has counterweights on the crankshaft. This includes most medium- and higher-horsepower lightplane engines. Because the counterweights have a pendulum action and must adjust to RPM changes, if you chop the throttle on one of these engines, the counterweight bushings can be ruined. Damaged counterweight bushings can lead to broken crankshafts. And that can lead you to the poorhouse at today's engine overhaul costs.

Student Attitude

Your attitude toward the learning process is extremely important as a student pilot—and for the rest of your flying career, for that matter. There is no such thing as a "born pilot" (except those that hatch from eggs). Good pilots don't just happen, they develop—properly directed— through the application of serious effort. That effort is sustained by a strong desire (need?) to excel, along with whatever other factors there may be that mark the high achiever. Your instructor can't give it to you. You bring it with you to the airport if you have it.

If you are a male, I hope that you will resist any tendency to assume the role of a strong, silent type. This usually masks a fear of making an embarrassing mistake or asking a "silly" question. And this is why some instructors will tell you that women often make better flight students than men. Most women aren't afraid to ask a "silly" question; and when they blow a maneuver they merely shrug it off and try again. They are not embarrassed by learning errors. No one should be. In ground school, a lot of student pilots are secretly grateful for the one who has the courage to ask the "silly" questions. They, too, need the answers, but don't ask because they don't want to reveal their ignorance. We are all ignorant of subjects new to us. There should be no embarrassment in that.

2

The
Traffic Pattern

A LOT OF AIRPLANES ARE DESTROYED IN AIRPORT TRAFFIC PATTERNS. A few of these are lost to midair collisions, but most stall in steep turns and plunge to the ground with the pilots holding full up-elevator. A flight instructor I know—I'll call him Ed—says that these crashes occur because traffic patterns are close to the ground. At first, I thought he was joking. He was having a postflight discussion with one of his students, a pleasant young man by the name of Don, and I was an interested bystander.

"You don't believe me?" Ed asked. "Then how come, in good weather, pilots only stall and spin in turns close to the ground? They don't do it higher up."

Don, a senior from the local university, was wary. "If you stall at traffic pattern height," he replied carefully, "there probably isn't enough room to recover." He squinted thoughtfully and added, "Also, you're flying at a lower airspeed in the pattern."

My instructor friend nodded agreement. "You've correctly identified two factors that contribute to the high fatality rate in the pattern. But what, specifically, makes some traffic pattern turns so dangerous? What are those pilots doing with the controls that they would not do at altitude?"

"Well," Don replied tentatively, "the only thing I can think of is that they might hurry a turn and mess it up."

Ed's smile was wide and beautiful. "Exactly! They are making a turn in relation to a fixed reference on the surface—the runway—and when they discover that they have waited too long to initiate the turn, they try to rack the airplane around in a steep turn." (See Fig. 2-1.)

"And that requires a lot of back pressure on the control wheel," Don added, "too much for that airspeed."

"That's most of it," Ed said, obviously proud of his student. "But also consider the position of the other flight controls. The pilot is holding a lot of rudder in the direction of the turn attempting to hurry the turn rate, while holding opposite aileron to counter the airplane's overbanking tendency. He is therefore set up for a particularly violent stall. Usually, the airplane will whip inverted and dive into the ground."

Fig. 2-1. Poor judgment; here we are trying to salvage an approach after misjudging the base-to-final turn in a right-hand pattern.

I left them at that point, thinking to myself that Ed's original statement about traffic patterns being close to the ground really had little to do with the discussion. Then it occurred to me that Ed had used it as an attention-getter. Frankly, I had always regarded Ed as being a mite on the windy side, but now I took another look at him. He had shared a carefully reasoned explanation with his student and caused his student to think—and that is the mark of a good teacher. Ed is also one of those flight instructors who recommend spin training to their students.

Spins

Spins are a part of U.S. military flight training programs and always have been, and spin training was taken for granted by all U.S. civilian instructors for many years. Back in the 1930s student pilots were required to demonstrate spin recovery before they were allowed to solo. The laws of physics do not change, so why is spin training no longer required in civilian flight training programs?

There are two different theories on this subject. One holds that spin training is without value (or, at least, unnecessary) because, if you are properly instructed in stall recovery techniques, you will never allow a stall to progress into a spin. Also, because the killer stalls are mostly those entered close to the ground, especially in airport traffic patterns, stall prevention is more important than spin recovery.

The other theory is that spins scared away too many students and potential students.

I believe that you should know how to recover from any unusual flight condition, including an inadvertent spin. If you have not experienced the entire sequence of events in each kind of stall (and its aftermath), you'll never know the full consequences of stalls and how to react to them. This, in turn, can lead to apprehension and doubt at a most inconvenient time.

Personally, I've never understood why the FAA changed its position with regard to spin training. The training wasn't dangerous. Back in the 1920s, before sophisticated instruments and instrument flying procedures were developed, airmail pilots caught above an overcast with fuel running low deliberately spun their big DH-4 biplanes down through the soup and hoped for enough ceiling to allow recovery in clear air. A spin was a known condition, with a relatively slow rate of descent, and it imposed no unusual stresses on the airframe. The wings on one side of the airplane were stalled, and the machine was in a stabilized descent.

In a typical civilian pilot training program, you will encounter only gentle stalls. With power at idle and the wheel all the way back, the average two-place trainer will mush along, bobbing its nose trying to find a flyable angle of attack, and although your VSI will confirm that you are losing altitude, you can rock the wings by turning the control wheel—which is proof enough that you aren't fully stalled. Some instructors will allow you to use the ailerons to pick up a wing if it drops in this situation. You can get by with this for years in a lightly loaded trainer, but it is a dangerous habit to take with you into airplanes with higher wing loadings. If a wing tends to drop in a stall, pick it up with opposite rudder.

Pattern Practices

You have a lot of latitude in planning the size and shape of the pattern you choose to fly during a landing approach, even at controlled airports (Fig. 2-2). The FARs do not describe a landing pattern (91.87 and 91.89) beyond mentioning that any turns are to be made to the left, unless, due to safety or noise abatement considerations, a right-hand pattern is indicated. The FAA does describe recommended traffic pattern procedures in Paragraphs 220–224 of the *Airman's Information Manual (AIM)*.

Fig. 2-2. Typical airport traffic pattern. *(Copyright 1986 Jeppesen Sanderson, Inc. Reprinted with permission.)*

Pattern altitude may extend from 600 to 1,500 feet above ground level (AGL), but 1,000 feet is recommended unless "established otherwise." (We are talking about propeller-driven lightplanes; jets will fly a higher pattern.)

Enter the pattern in level flight at cruising airspeed approximately midway along the downwind leg (earlier in higher-speed aircraft). Enter at a 45-degree angle in order to best observe other traffic. If you must turn away from the pattern to keep from crowding another airplane, make a 360-degree turn away from the pattern. Do the same if you are in the pattern, have the right-of-way, and someone else comes crowding in. He probably doesn't see you. Once in a while you will encounter a nerf brain who will cut you off in the pattern at an uncontrolled field. When you do, the same drill applies; give him room, and remind yourself that it's better to have the idiots in front when you can see them rather than behind where you can't. Remember, whenever you decide to do a 360 advise the tower in advance, or at an uncontrolled field, announce your intentions on the Common Traffic Advisory Frequency (CTAF).

Keep in mind while making *any* turn near an airport that you have a big blind spot either above or below your airplane, depending upon where your wing is located (Fig. 2-3).

Maintain the pattern altitude on the downwind leg (Fig. 2-4) until you are abeam of the approach end of the landing runway. Continue on the downwind leg as appropriate to the conditions, normally between ¼ and ¾ of a mile. Wind velocity and other traffic are the principal factors that will determine the length of your downwind leg. Traffic permitting, many pilots begin their turns to the base leg (Fig. 2-5) when the runway threshold is about 45° behind.

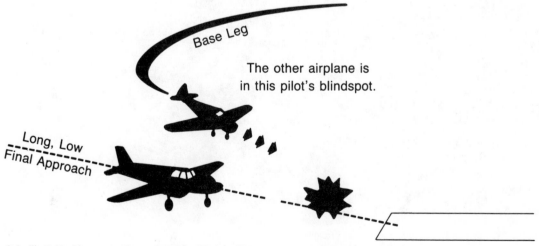

Base Leg

The other airplane is
in this pilot's blindspot.

Long, Low
Final Approach

Fig. 2-3. Illustrated is a recurring cause of mid-air collisions in the traffic pattern at uncontrolled airports.

Fig. 2-4. Downwind at cruising speed.

Fig. 2-5. Base leg. There's another Cessna trainer behind us in the pattern, but we haven't seen him since he left the runway and he is not transmitting his position/intentions on the CTAF frequency as we are.

Plan your turn to the final approach so that when you complete the turn you will be properly aligned with the runway, and at least ¼ mile from the threshold (Figs. 2-6 through 2-9). If you are landing at an airport which has parallel runways, make sure that you do not overshoot your turn to final and intrude into the approach airspace of the parallel runway.

On takeoff, if you are departing the pattern, continue straight ahead or exit with a 45-degree left turn (right turn if a right-hand pattern) beyond the departure end of the runway after reaching pattern altitude.

If you are remaining in the pattern, begin your turn to the crosswind leg beyond the departure end of the runway and within 300 feet of pattern altitude.

In planning your pattern, allow for some flexibility to compensate for varying wind and traffic conditions. This flexibility is gained by flying a tighter or looser pattern. If, for example, you are landing into a strong wind, your turn to the base leg will be made sooner than usual and your final approach will be shorter. Wind, visibility, traffic, terrain, and even a housing development below can modify that turn to the base leg.

As for those built-up areas around an airport, it is ironic that they followed the airport, which originally sat out there in splendid isolation. The airport created jobs, which in turn created a shopping center and new housing. Once the newcomers were settled, they began complaining

Fig. 2-6. Final approach. This is Altus (Oklahoma) Municipal Airport. There are two more airplanes on the taxiway.

Fig. 2-7. We will touchdown just beyond the numbers.

Fig. 2-8. Looks like we cheated death once again, but we shouldn't brag too much, rolling out this far to the right of the centerline.

about the noise and low-flying aircraft. I know of at least two modern runways at major air terminals that are no longer used because of complaints from the neighbors. It's human nature, I suppose, and there isn't much you can do about it except try to get along—they greatly outnumber you.

Tower-Controlled Airports

If you are a beginning pilot flying from an airport with an operating control tower, you may have despaired of ever understanding a word of the metallic directives emanating from the overhead radio speaker in the airplane. Not only are the controllers' words unintelligible, but you may be one of those who regard the use of the radio communication with much apprehension. If this is the case, the best suggestion I can offer is: Relax. The use of your comm radio is one of those relatively simple things that can seem difficult when you try too hard.

You will find it easier to relax if you know what you are doing. The controllers' transmissions become much easier to understand once you become aware of the standardized sequence he or she is required to use. Therefore, we will discuss in detail your communications with the controllers in Chapter 7. Proper use of your radio is an integral part of your landing and takeoff operations—including operations from uncontrolled airports.

Visual Airport Indicators

At many airports, largely those which are uncontrolled or controlled part-time, you will find a segmented circle near the runway with a wind indicator in its center and traffic pattern direction indicators outside the circle. The wind direction indicator may be the time-honored wind sock (Fig. 2-9) or a wind tee. The tee's cross-bar end points into the wind, as does the fat part of the wind sock. Sometimes, if the wind tee has a wind sock mounted on it or nearby, the tee is manually anchored to indicate the runway in use.

Anytime you have a wind sock for reference, use it. It is the best and most reliable wind direction indicator. It also provides a clue as to wind velocity. Occasionally, you will see a tetrahedron, which resembles the delta-shaped paper airplanes you used to sail in study hall. The pointy end of the tetrahedron points in the landing direction; that is, it will be aligned with the active. It is not a wind indicator.

Outside the segmented circle you may find traffic pattern indicators, sometimes omitted at airports with the standard left-hand pattern. Pattern direction indicators will always be displayed if a right-hand pattern is in use, even when no segmented circle is evident.

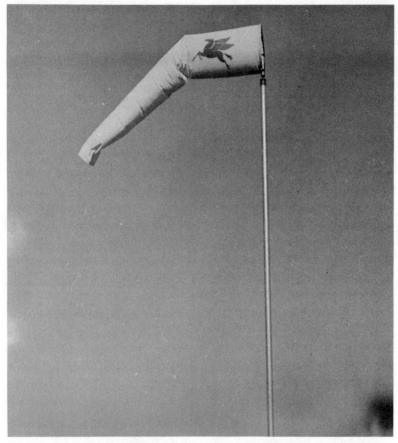

Fig. 2-9. Sometimes you have to search to find the wind sock. The large end points into the wind.

The Low Level Wind
Shear Alert System (LLWAS)

At some of the larger controlled airports the tower controller will provide wind shear alerts to arriving and departing aircraft when appropriate. At these airports—identified in the *Airport/Facility Directory*—a system of sensors around the airport boundary electronically compares wind data with a sensor near the airport's center to indicate conditions which may result in significant wind shears.

Intersection Takeoffs

Intersection takeoffs may be approved, and even initiated, by controllers in order to speed up traffic flow at busy airports.

Controllers are supposed to separate aircraft of 12,500 pounds or less which are taking off from an intersection behind a large or heavy aircraft (see "aircraft classes" in the Glossary) on the same runway by ensuring at least a three-minute interval between the time the large or heavy airplane has taken off and the small airplane begins its takeoff. The controller will usually tell you that you are being held for wake turbulence. If you're the adventurous (i.e. stupid) type, you can tell the controller that you want to waive the three-minute interval, and if the other aircraft isn't a "heavy" the controller may clear you because you have accepted responsibility for the possible crash.

The three-minute interval rule does not apply when the intersection is 500 feet or less from the runway threshold and the "small" plane is taking off behind a "large" plane. The interval is mandatory behind "heavy" aircraft in all cases.

Lights

At night, or in low visibility situations, strobes and/or rotating anticollision lights on your airplane should be turned on anytime your engine is operating on the ground—but this is a judgment call. The FAA says turn 'em on to comply with their "Operation Lights On" program, and FAR 91.73 says you turn 'em off "in the interest of safety" if they adversely affect your own or others' vision. You are encouraged to turn on your landing lights when flying within 10 miles of an airport, day or night, in conditions of reduced visibility. Be sure to check the manufacturer's recommendations for the operation of your landing lights.

You are aware, of course, that your position (navigation) lights must be turned on anytime your engine is operating between sunset and sunrise, but you'd be wise to *always* have them on.

Collision Avoidance

Since the early 1960s, there has been some talk about—and some lackadaisical research into—electronic anticollision systems for aircraft. The development was slowed because the FAA wanted to operate any such system, while the airline pilots' union, ALPA, (probably the most influential civil aviation lobby in Washington) insisted that the system adopted should consist of airborne units and that ATC controllers should be cut out of the loop.

It appears that ALPA has prevailed. Piedmont began tests of an airborne unit in 1981, and United began installing the TCAS II (Traffic Alert and Collision Avoidance System) in February 1987. Built by Bendix (which also owns Martin-Marietta), and by Sperry (purchased by Burroughs in 1986), the TCAS II is said to be priced at $80,000 per installation. It is a compact radar that interrogates all nearby transponder-equipped aircraft fitted with encoding altimeters (Mode C capability).

The display shows where the electronically queried targets are in relation to the TCAS II-equipped airliner, and the returning signal also provides altitude information as a result of the encoding altimeter interface (just as it does for ground controllers).

This system is certain to be developed and refined, and the future impact on general aviation will be additional pressure for Mode C capability for all. In fact, several FAA Notices of Proposed Rule Making (NPRMs) in circulation at this writing signal the beginning of this new era.

Whatever the rules and restrictions, the safe separation of airborne aircraft is the primary purpose of ATC. Almost all mid-airs and near misses occur in the vicinity of an airport. There is sufficient possibility of mid-air collisions to make the subject one of concern, although the news media have greatly overstated it. Actually, the FAA said there were 141 "near misses" in 1986 in which two airplanes appeared to come within 100 feet of one another in flight. This was stretched into a total of 828 by including those occasions considered "dangerously close" (up to five miles—five miles being the separation the controllers attempt to maintain between airplanes).

Controllers and electronic wizardry notwithstanding, the final responsibility for inflight collision avoidance rests with the pilots, and the practical protection you can give to yourself and those "near" to you in the air includes:

1. Be alert to the truly dangerous situations, such as a long final approach that could allow you to let down on top of an airplane hidden from your view by the nose of your machine. Also keep in mind as you turn onto final from base leg that another airplane on an extended final approach may be blocked from your view. At uncontrolled fields, another pilot may try to enter the pattern on a short base leg, and he, too, would be blocked from your view as you turn from downwind to base leg. The turn from base leg to final approach is probably the most dangerous turn in all of flying because the attention of most pilots is directed at the runway in order to achieve good alignment for the final approach. Here is where it's easy to stall the airplane with crossed controls while hurrying the turn rate, and here is where we tend to be the least observant of other traffic. So the first rule is *vigilance*, and that includes your scan, both inside and outside. Take in as much of the sky as you can, along with frequent checks of the airspeed indicator, turn coordinator, and attitude indicator.

2. The second rule has got to be *compliance*—compliance with the rules and standard procedures. The primary purpose of a traffic pattern is the order, or the basis for order, that it imposes on airport traffic. Honor it, and do what everyone

else has the right to expect that you will do. It's not enough
that you avoid other traffic; you must *be* avoided as well.

Some pilots are uncertain as to how or where to enter traffic patterns
at uncontrolled fields when approaching from any direction except one
which takes them directly into the downwind leg. First, plan a minimal
amount of maneuvering above or outside the pattern. For example, if
your cross-country course terminates on the non-pattern side of the
airport, maintain at least 1,500 feet altitude AGL and fly across the airport
above pattern altitude. Continue above and across the pattern, beyond
the normal track of the downwind leg, then let down to pattern altitude
and turn (to the right in a left-hand pattern, to the left in a right-hand
pattern)—normally about 225°—so that you enter the downwind leg at
the usual 45-degree angle.

You may, of course, simply enter the upwind leg and fly the crosswind
and entire downwind, if you choose. The reason for overflying a strange
airport is to find the wind indicator and make sure of the runway in use
before entering the pattern.

If your approach to your destination airport is toward the crosswind
leg (upwind of the active), it's best to make a shallow turn before reaching
the pattern altitude so that you can enter the downwind leg, making sure
that you are not crowding anyone who may be in the pattern on upwind
or crosswind making touch-and-gos. The only thing wrong with a long
straight-in track to the downwind leg is that it falls into the category of
the unexpected. If you choose to enter the pattern that way, be especially
alert for aircraft which may enter the downwind ahead of you, and always
announce your intentions on the CTAF.

It is always best to plan your pattern to allow shallow turns; and you
must never enter a pattern upwind of the departure end of the runway.
An airplane below your altitude which has just become airborne can be
very hard to see. Preliminary planning for a proper entry to a traffic
pattern at a strange uncontrolled airport should be made prior to takeoff
with a check of the *Airport/Facility Directory*.

Try not to allow the transgressions of others to influence your own
procedures. There will always be a minority of selfish, self-centered
people in all human endeavors, including flying. Occasionally, you will
be cut off in the pattern, and you will have to give way to some character
with an inventive nature. I once saw a pilot fly the base leg in an opposite
direction (that's how he entered the pattern), and then do a tight
270-degree turn onto a short final. He was flying (if that's the word for
it) a Temco Swift, and he needed every inch of the 4,500-foot runway.
He was dressed like the Red Baron, and clearly was just as dangerous.
He was also almost completely out of fuel.

Spacing and Wake Turbulence

At controlled airports, tower will take care of the spacing between aircraft; that's the controllers' primary job. But that does not relieve you of the responsibility of avoiding other aircraft as well as their wake turbulence. You will often be reminded of that. As of this writing, it appears that wake turbulence may have been a factor in a tragic airliner crash on the runway at Denver in November 1987. Another airliner landed on a parallel runway 1,500 feet away within three minutes prior to the ill-fated liner's attempted takeoff, according to early reports.

It's unlikely that you will encounter wake turbulence from a heavy aircraft at an uncontrolled airport, but this invisible danger is spawned by all fixed-wing airplanes, its severity being a matter of degree. I had not planned to say much about wake turbulence here because I believed that, surely, everyone had the word on it by this time. I personally haven't heard of a lightplane pilot falling victim to it since a factory test Cessna Skymaster crashed in the wake turbulence of an Air Force jet fighter at Wichita several years ago, but in the light of recent developments, perhaps I should try to clearly define this insidious danger.

The main source of the turbulence formed in the wake of fixed-wing airplanes in flight has its genesis in the pressure differential between the air flowing over the top of the wing and that flowing under the bottom of the wing. The pressure beneath is much greater, and this results in the air beneath the wing spilling over the wingtips toward the lower pressure, while the forward motion of the aircraft causes it to roll up in the airflow behind the wing. The ultimate effect is a pair of counter-rotating cylindrical vortices—one streaming back from each wingtip—which resemble miniature horizontal tornadoes (Fig. 2-10).

The strength of these vortices depends upon the weight and speed of the aircraft, along with the shape of the wing. The behavior of these vortices is affected by extension of flaps and leading-edge slats, as well as by a change in speed. The FAA says that the basic factor is weight; the vortex strength increases proportionately with aircraft weight. During tests, peak vortex tangential velocities were recorded at 224 feet per second, or about 133 knots. The greatest vortex strength occurs when the generating aircraft is *heavy, clean*, and *slow*.

The vortices, a by-product of lift, begin from the instant the aircraft becomes airborne, and cease at the point of touchdown (Fig. 2-11). Vortices close to the ground tend to move laterally at a speed of about four knots, and their movement will be modified by the wind. Because the vortices from heavy airplanes sink at the rate of about 400–500 feet per minute, you must be aware that they can sink into traffic patterns

WAKE TURBULENCE

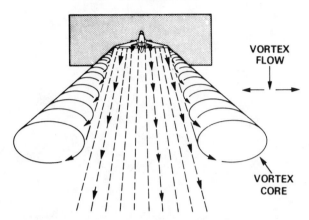

Fig. 2-10. Wake turbulence; the greatest vortex strength occurs when the generating aircraft is heavy, clean, and slow.

from other operations, or into your takeoff or landing path from an intersecting runway.

In view of the above, there are a few simple rules you can follow to stay clear of potential wake turbulence problems:

- If you follow a large or heavy category aircraft on takeoff, you should lift off prior to its point of rotation, then remain above and upwind of its flight path until you turn clear of its wake.

- Following a large or heavy aircraft on landing, remain at or above its final approach path, and land beyond its touchdown point.

At controlled airports the controllers will provide wake turbulence cautions when they believe it appropriate, and will maintain a distance of six miles between a heavy aircraft and a following lightplane landing on the same runway or on parallel runways less than 2,500 feet apart.

For takeoff, the separation is a minimum of two minutes or four miles between a heavy aircraft and a following small aircraft from the same runway (a five-mile separation from intersecting runways) and when parallel runways are less than 2,500 feet apart.

Note that the takeoff separation is two minutes *or* four miles (radar measurement). You may ask the controller for the two minutes rather than the four miles. On a calm day that may not leave you feeling comfortable about the situation.

Be aware that a helicopter in forward flight produces vortices in its wake similar to those created by fixed-wing aircraft.

Fig. 2-11. When departing behind a heavy arrival, lift off beyond his touchdown point.

Hurry-Up Approaches

At controlled fields the tower may ask you to "expedite" a directive from the controller, and/or "make a short approach." Expedite means do it *now*; and the directive to make a short approach refers to your final approach. You may be told to make a straight-in approach, or to enter the pattern on base leg. Gusty conditions can argue for an approach speed higher than your normal 1.3 times stall speed, as can a wind shear warning. Usually, however, the need to speed up your approach is due to the fact that you are sharing the pattern with faster airplanes.

First, let's consider an ATC-directed straight-in approach. Where should you be, when, and at what speed? (Suddenly, you appreciate the stylized pattern, where you have guidelines for everything.) You are going to arbitrarily select a starting point or key position from which to set up your approach. Let's make it two miles from the threshold of the active. You will let down so as to reach pattern altitude at that point, with your pre-landing chores tidied up.

Begin your let-down from that point with a reduction in power and partial flaps. With elevator pressure and trim adjust airspeed to 60 knots in our Cessna Aerobat (it stalls at 45 knots IAS with flaps and idle power), which translates roughly into two minutes to the runway threshold, depending upon the wind, and that suggests a 500-FPM descent. These are estimates because (1) ground speed is going to determine your actual time to the runway, (2) your two-mile key position was a guess, and (3) you are not going to shoot for the threshold, but about halfway down the first third of the runway.

You can now crank down full flaps, trim off the elevator pressure once again, and watch your intended touchdown point in relation to a fixed reference spot on your windshield in order to determine whether the intended touchdown point moves above or below that reference as your approach progresses.

If the reference spot on the windshield (some instructors make a grease-pencil mark on the windshield) appears to move down in relation to the desired point on the runway, you are going to land short of that point; therefore, add power. It won't take much.

If the reference spot on your windshield is moving above the planned touchdown point, you are going to land beyond it, in which case, back off the throttle. Remember, control the rate of descent with power, and control airspeed with pitch.

If the controller has directed that you enter the pattern on base leg, you should be at pattern altitude when you begin that base with the threshold approximately 45° off the nose of your airplane. From that point, complete a normal approach. But if this directive is accompanied by a request that you "make a short approach," then fly the base leg so that your turn onto final will be made about ¼ mile from the threshold.

At controlled airports where there is no congestion, and at uncontrolled airports where there are no special procedures, fly a good standard pattern—one that will give you plenty of time to concentrate on your landing. It will eliminate the need to catch up with the airplane with last-minute trim and speed corrections. A good final approach distance in single-engine lightplanes under normal conditions is about ½ mile—a little longer for retractables.

At uncontrolled airports, a good rule of thumb for lightplane separation is the length of the runway on takeoff, the length of a pattern leg in the pattern, and the decision to go around halfway down final if the active runway is not cleared by then. There will be times when you will get boxed-in between two other planes in the pattern and will need to extend your downwind leg to maintain sufficient approach spacing. The more planes in the pattern, the larger the pattern will grow, but there's not much an individual plane can do about this other than abandoning the pattern and heading to another field.

I haven't gone into detail yet on the use of radios because I agree with those instructors who believe that a student will progress faster and retain more if not overwhelmed with too many new concepts at once.

The conventional wisdom among professional educators holds that an instructor should introduce no more than four new concepts or procedures per week to the average student. That is why some flight instructors prefer to wait until their students have absorbed those first few hours of dual instruction before giving them the responsibility of handling the airborne radiotelephone with its special language.

3

Over the Fence

THE FINAL APPROACH IS AS MUCH A PART OF THE LANDING AS IT IS A PART of the airport traffic pattern. That's what flight instructions mean when they say, "Good landings start with good approaches."

In a sense, the downwind and base legs are also parts of the landing. On downwind, which is flown at normal cruising speed, apply carburetor heat and take a good look at the airport in general, the active runway in particular, and any taxiing aircraft that might need watching. (I once had a Continental Airlines Convair swing onto the runway and take off at then-uncontrolled Lawton (Oklahoma) Municipal Airport as I was turning final in a Luscombe with a failed engine. I remember wishing aloud that he would bust his next physical.)

On the downwind leg, be conscious of the runway's position parallel to your flight path and use it to detect any drifting of your machine toward or away from it. Precision, remember?

Any wind effect that you notice at initial pattern altitude is not necessarily duplicated on the surface, but it can be a clue. Wind usually increases with altitude, and normally "backs" to come from a more westerly direction.

As the runway threshold passes your left wingtip (assuming a left-hand pattern), reduce power and adjust the fuel mixture to the full rich position. On our Cessna trainer, 10° of flaps is optional at this point as the airspeed permits flap deployment. Later, as you move up to more complex aircraft, there will be more to do. You will have a pre-landing checklist that includes a booster pump, and a wastegate to open (on turbocharged engines), along with propeller pitch control, which goes to high RPM setting after the airplane has slowed to its approach speed.

When the runway threshold appears to be about 45° behind your left wing, make your turn to base leg. Leveling the wings on base, you can further reduce power if necessary, and hold the nose up with elevator until your airspeed slows to near final approach speed. You'll need a bit of left rudder to counteract the decrease in torque. Nearing final approach speed (60–65 knots in a typical trainer), add another notch of flaps and maintain your desired speed with pitch. Speed control is the key to a good approach. Most pilots carry too much airspeed down final. The figures given in the owner's manual are predicated on maximum gross weight; yet you seldom land at that weight. With the airspeed stabilized, re-trim, and don't forget your complete scan. Particularly, look off your outside wing for any aircraft that may be making a long final. At uncontrolled airports, commuter airlines like to make such approaches.

Your turn to the final approach leg is a descending turn with a shallow bank—repeat, *shallow*, like 30° in smooth air; perhaps 15° in turbulence (Fig. 3-1). You will probably have to "play" this turn to compensate for any wind that is not directly down the runway. Your immediate object, of course, is to line up with the runway centerline. Wait until you are sure that you can reach the runway before lowering full flaps. Flaps will significantly increase your angle of descent, and it is best not to deploy full flaps too soon because once they are down, retracting them to stretch an approach can be dangerous. You should only stretch your approach with your throttle.

In fact, it is unlikely that you will be able to continue a landing approach with power at idle unless there is no wind. A stabilized power setting down final might be desired, but in most cases a number of things intrude which require an increase or decrease in the power setting to adjust your rate of descent. With your touchdown spot matched to a spot on your windshield, you keep it there with light touches of power or power reduction.

If you find that wind is drifting you to one side or the other of the runway centerline (Fig. 3-2), drop the appropriate wing into the wind with aileron, while maintaining a straight track down the centerline with opposite rudder. This is, of course, a very gentle, prolonged slip. Maintain airspeed with pitch and rate of descent with power as usual. However, if the crosswind component requires that you carry the upwind wing quite low, you might not have enough rudder to keep the airplane's longitudinal axis aligned with the runway's centerline as speed erodes during the flare.

Fig. 3-1. Turning from base leg to final approach at an airport using a right-hand pattern. Runway threshold is about ¾ mile away, and your altitude is 700 feet AGL.

Therefore, if you've got the upwind wing down pretty far and a lot of rudder is needed to maintain track, consider going around and landing on a different runway—even if it means going to another airport.

At controlled airports, you will have the surface wind conditions from the tower or ATIS, and your owner's manual will list the maximum allowable crosswind, which is one of the numbers you should know before flying. Allow a little for gusts, your experience level, and the condition of your airplane (the numbers in your owner's manual were established by a highly competent test pilot flying a brand-new airplane at gross weight in "standard atmosphere conditions," that is, corrected to sea level and 59° F, unless otherwise noted).

At uncontrolled airports you are forced to judge the surface wind from the appearance of the windsock and whatever other clues you can observe. As a rule, you shouldn't place too much faith in UNICOM weather observations. I will discuss crosswind landings in more detail momentarily.

Fig. 3-2. Line up with the runway centerline, but wait until you are sure that you have the runway made before lowering full flaps. You are a little to the right of the centerline and a bit low. Add a touch of power.

Forward Slips

Back in the open-cockpit biplane days, fliers had neither flaps nor any suspicion that they needed them. On final approach, they performed forward slips to get rid of excess altitude without picking up unwanted airspeed. The hot pilots often slipped both ways. Wing flaps have proven a lot more practical and, surely, safer. There is, however, still a need to master the forward slip. It can be a real lifesaver if you ever have to shoehorn your flying machine into a small field somewhere with a failed engine. And you must be able to demonstrate an acceptable forward slip on your flight tests.

The slip is a simple maneuver, but it contains a possible danger for the unwary. During a slip the relative wind is entering the pitot head at an angle and your airspeed indicator is not giving you an accurate reading. So the slip is, to a great extent, a seat-of-the-pants maneuver. Simply put a wing down in the direction of the slip (with aileron) and apply opposite rudder. The longitudinal axis of the airplane is yawed at an angle to the runway centerline, but your ground track remains aligned with the centerline. The amount of rudder needed will vary with the bank angle.

Exactly where along your approach the slip is established will depend upon the situation. Unfortunately, pilots often wait until the need is unmistakable—usually on short final. Termination of the slip is also a judgment call. Don't overdo this maneuver. If a moderate slip is not sufficient, it's time to think about a go-around. The belated need for a forward slip is in itself a good indication of poor planning. Don't attempt to salvage a poorly planned approach.

In a slip, the wings lose significant lift because of the change in relative wind; this results in a loss of altitude. But, because of the extra drag produced by the airplane's sideways attitude, the airplane does not pick up airspeed. Meanwhile, you must hold some back pressure on the control wheel to prevent airspeed from increasing.

As I said, it is a seat-of-the-pants maneuver, and you can see where the danger lurks for inexperienced pilots. You enter the slip from approach airspeed, you are close to the ground, your controls are crossed, you are holding the nose up with the elevator, and you are referencing an uncertain airspeed indicator. Good grief!

Actually, it isn't as bad as it sounds, because you are only a couple of seconds from returning the airplane to its normal approach configuration. To do this, simultaneously level the wings and return the rudder to neutral. Continue to hold a little back pressure on the control wheel as required for airspeed control. The secret of a good slip is to hold just the right amount of up-elevator—just enough to keep the nose from dropping. Too much, of course, could stall the airplane.

Never slip in gusty wind conditions or over approach terrain that could generate orographic turbulence. Check the airplane's owner's manual for any prohibition of slips, including slips with flaps deployed. For years, pilots were told they must not slip a Cessna trainer with its flap down. Cessna later changed that to say it was "not recommended." Flap travel is limited to 30° on late-model Cessna 152s, and slips are acceptable.

Return to Earth

Don't hurry the flare (Figs. 3-3 through 3-5). Up to this point you have accomplished two-thirds of the landing; the rest is going to fall into place if you have done everything right so far. As you reach the height above the runway where the flare is begun (a good estimate is one-half the plane's wingspan, or 12-15 feet in a light single-engine airplane), start to apply back pressure on the control wheel to further slow the airplane.

Fig. 3-3. This is a controlled airport, and controllers appreciate precision, especially when things get busy, but you are a little high and will not make that first exit. Don't dive for the runway; just let it roll and catch the next taxiway.

Fig. 3-4. Focus your eyes well ahead of the airplane for the flare.

Fig. 3-5. Here is how you looked in the flare.

Do this as slowly and steadily as possible. In practice, you can judge when to start the flare by looking as far ahead as you would if driving a car at the same speed. If you look too far down the runway, you will have a tendency to flare too late and too low. If you don't look far enough down the runway, or look to the side, you will tend to flare too high.

Power should be at idle when you begin the flare. What you are trying to do is hold the airplane off the runway as long as you possibly can with pitch alone. Expect to run out of up-elevator travel as the airplane stalls at about one foot above the surface. If you see that you are going to stall while still several feet in the air, release a little back pressure. If you are settling too fast, feed in a touch of power, but make no large control or power changes; it takes a light touch here. If you feel the mains touch before the control wheel is all the way back, do not yank the wheel back to catch up; just continue to smoothly and steadily bring it on back to the stops.

A precipitous decrease in pitch as the airplane settles those final few feet will almost certainly result in a bounce, the severity of which will depend upon the sink rate. Do not attempt to correct a bounce by shoving the control wheel forward. Just feed in a touch of power, keep the nose high (you don't want the nosewheel to touch first), and allow your machine to settle gently.

With the mains rolling, maintain a straight track down the runway centerline with the rudder, and hold the nosewheel off as long as you can. As speed dissipates, the nosewheel will gently lower on its own accord. Do not use brakes until the nosewheel is down. There are several advantages in doing it this way when conditions permit: (1) with the nose high, you are getting effective aerodynamic braking from the wings during the first third of the rollout, thereby reducing brake wear; (2) you are saving wear on the nosewheel tire and the rather weak—and expensive—nosewheel shimmy dampener on Cessnas, and (3) you are relieving a good deal of stress on the nose gear attach points. Even though you might not be directly paying for the maintenance on a training airplane, the day might come when you own your own flying machine, so maintenance-saving habits are useful ones to acquire.

The full-stall landing is also easier on the main landing gear and tires. All those black tire marks on the first third of the runway are "spin-up" marks, put down during the split-second of main-gear touchdown, when tire rotation accelerates from zero to touchdown velocity. You not only leave a little rubber on the concrete every time you land, but you also place a significant rearward force on the landing gear struts and their attachment areas. Lightplanes are normally designed to withstand a rearward force on their main gear that is 20% greater than that imposed when touching down at stall speed. Land faster than that and you risk permanent distortion of the landing gear attachment area. On the other hand, you can drop the airplane onto the runway from two or three feet in a full-stall landing without damaging the structure.

Many pilots like to raise the flaps as soon as the main wheels are on the runway in order to decrease lift, transfer weight to the wheels, and to improve the ground steering ability after the nosewheel comes down. But most instructors seem to frown on this practice. They say that it's easy to fumble around and grab the wrong control (perhaps raising the landing gear instead of the flaps), when your attention is required outside of the cockpit during rollout. They maintain this position despite the fact that most flap controls are shaped like a flap and most landing gear controls are shaped like a wheel. The problem, of course, is Murphy's Law, said to have been promulgated by the pilot of the first retractable-gear airplane in 1921.

As speed dissipates during the landing rollout, remain alert and sensitive to any tendency of the airplane to deviate from its straight track. A lot of aircraft have been bent on landing rollout because their pilots simply "quit payin' attention." Remember the ancient and hallowed saying: "You are flying it until it's in the hangar."

Visual Approach Slope Indicator

Many airports have a Visual Approach Slope Indicator (VASI), a system of lights located near the runway threshold (usually on the left side, sometimes on both sides), which provides pilots with a visual glide slope reference. There are several versions of this system, containing from 2-16 lights. All serve the same purpose - to aid you in maintaining a safe and proper glide path. They provide safe obstruction clearance within $\pm 10°$ of the extended runway centerline, and up to 4 NM from the runway threshold. Two-bar VASIs give lightplanes a three-degree approach path. Three-bar installations serve lightplanes with the near set of lights and airliners (high cockpits) with the middle and far sets of lights. Some VASI installations have glide slopes of up to $4\frac{1}{2}°$ for safe obstacle clearance.

The basic principle of these systems is color differentiation between red and white. Each light projects a beam with a white segment in the upper part and a red segment in the lower part of the beam. Red above and white below means that you are on the glide path. All red indicates that you are low, and all white means that you are too high.

Other types of visual approach slope systems are based on a single light unit. One of these is tri-color: amber if you are above the glide path, red if you are below, and green if you are on the glide path. Dark amber might appear momentarily when the color changes from green to red. Another is a single-light unit that shows pulsating white when high, pulsating red when low, and a steady white or alternating red-and-white when on the glide path. This rather rare system can be mistaken for another airplane or ground vehicle at night, so use caution.

There is also a low-cost and very dependable system that consists of three plywood panels, usually painted black and white, or international orange (Fig. 3-6). To use this system, position you airplane so that the panels appear to be in lateral alignment (the center one is actually set behind the other two). If you are too high, the center panel will show "above" or farther away; if too low, the center panel will appear closer or "below" the other two. All such systems are pictured and described in detail in the *Airman's Information Manual*.

The Aborted Landing

Any number of things can dictate a balked landing—a final approach that is too high, spacing that is too tight, or an impossible directive from

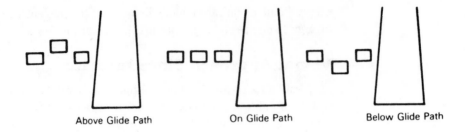

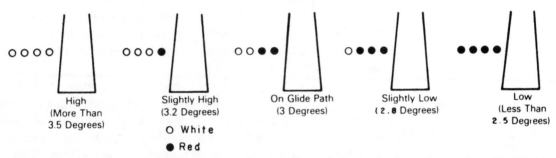

Fig. 3-6. The low-cost visual glideslope aid (top) consists of three plywood panels with the center one offset. The Precision Approach Path Indicator (PAPI, below) uses a color scheme similar to the VASI but with a single row of either two or four light units.

a controller. Final approach isn't the place to argue with a controller. Just say to him, "Tower, Cessna Two Seven Juliet. Unable to comply. Going around."

If Tower doesn't then give you specific instructions for a go-around, the procedure you will follow depends upon where you are in the pattern (I'll come to that). Meanwhile, you are completely within your rights to reject any ATC directive that could create a dangerous situation for you, or which is beyond your ability or experience level, or beyond the capability of your aircraft. If you are flying a Cessna 172 and Approach Control or Tower has sequenced you into the pattern ahead of a Learjet and then admonishes you to speed up, use common sense. Accommodate the bizjet and the controller to the extent that you safely can, but don't allow them to stampede you into a risky procedure. It may be possible for you to whistle over the fence at near double your normal approach speed and, if there is enough runway, smoke your binders to a stop before plowing through the opposite fence, but it is hardly sensible. Your common sense options, if you believe that you cannot significantly increase your speed and then land safely, are to let the jet go around while you complete your landing, or you may opt to go around instead—not because you are chicken, but as an act of courtesy. Perhaps you have noticed how, in the operation of our various machines, courtesy and safety go together.

The need to abort a landing usually becomes impossible to ignore by the time you are on short final. There is a temptation to postpone such a decision as long as possible, but good airmanship demands an early decision. The sooner you decide, the easier and safer it will be.

Assuming that you are on short final, with full flaps and partial power, apply full power and turn off the carburetor heat. Bring up the flaps to the setting recommended for go-around in the owner's manual (usually the same as a soft-field takeoff, which is 10° in the Cessna 150/152), but raise the flaps in 10-degree increments. Raising flaps reduces your lift, so don't bring them up all at once. With your aircraft in level attitude, briefly hold what you have until you pick up speed and re-trim, then establish your climb in the normal manner—hold level flight as speed builds and while you re-trim, then climb out at V_y or V_x (best rate or best angle) as conditions indicate. Make a left turn (if in a left-hand pattern) into the crosswind leg of the pattern, carefully scanning for other traffic.

Remember that power is your first consideration, and be prepared to counter the torque with rudder as you feed in full throttle. And if traffic is taking off on the runway below, fly to the right of, and parallel to, the runway so you can keep an eye on the traffic.

If a go-around is called for by a horrific bounce, the result of flaring too high—or perhaps not flaring at all—just remain calm, apply full power, go forward on the wheel to level flight attitude, carb heat to the cold position, and slowly bring the flaps up to the manufacturer's recommended setting for a go-around. You'll have to correct for torque, re-trim, and inform the controller of your intentions.

It isn't likely that you will find it necessary to abort a landing from the downwind or base leg of an airport traffic pattern, but it does happen, usually because someone does somethin' dumb. If pattern traffic is such that your 45-degree entry into the downwind leg might crowd another airplane, turn away to the right (in a left-hand pattern) and return for another try. If it's a controlled field, inform the tower; if it's an uncontrolled airport, transmit your intentions on the CTAF. If the airport is uncontrolled, you should already have the proper CTAF tuned, because you should have announced your intentions as you approached the field.

Crosswind Landings

It seems that almost everyone explains crosswind landings the same way. They tell you that there are two ways to handle such a situation, detail both, and then inform you that one of these methods should not be used. Sort of as an afterthought most add that a combination of the two methods—the crabbing or "kickout" method, and the wing-low method—is often used.

Employing the crabbing method, you establish the amount of crab necessary to counter the crosswind as you level off from the turn to final approach (Figs. 3-7 and 3-8). Unless the wind is gusting or there is the possibility of a wind shear, use normal approach airspeed and flaps (unless the owner's manual recommends otherwise). In gusty conditions, increase approach speed by half the amount of the gusts; that is, if you normally approach at 60 knots and the crosswind is 10 knots gusting to 20, increase your approach speed by at least 5 knots.

Maintaining a ground track by crabbing into the wind is a simple proposition, your crab angle dictated by wind velocity. Use common sense, however, along with the maximum crosswind figure given in the airplane's owner's manual. While you might be able to maintain your ground track in a strong crosswind, you might not have enough rudder available to "kick out" the crab angle for touchdown, and your landing gear is not designed to land sideways. Some years ago, Goodyear

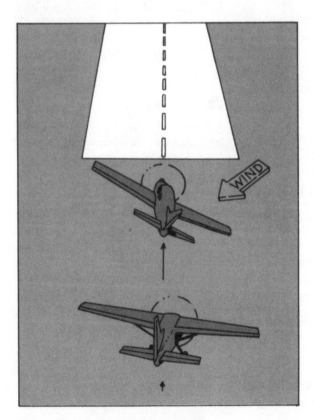

Fig. 3-7. Crab and slip methods of crosswind correction. *(Copyright 1986 Jeppesen Sanderson, Inc. Reprinted with permission.)*

Fig. 3-8. A strong crosswind from the right requires a substantial crab angle to keep the airplane tracking down the extended runway centerline on final. The approach is easier this way, but you can't afford to touchdown in this attitude. An instant before touch down the nose must be yawed straight ahead, quickly and accurately, which is why the wing-low method is usually preferred.

perfected a crosswind landing gear for tailwheel-type airplanes (Fig. 3-9). You maintained the crab right onto the runway and the main wheels castered to roll straight ahead, while you went sailing down the runway with the airplane pointed at the terminal building. That was an eerie sensation, and required a bit of faith.

Carry the crab angle right into the flare with this procedure, and at the last second before the wheels touch, yaw the nose to point straight down the runway. It is not easy because, clearly, you must apply exactly the right amount of rudder. (You do not "kick" the rudder pedal any more than you "slam" a control stick forward. Those terms are for fiction stories.) If you try this method as a student pilot, what you may feel like kicking is your own backside for thinking that you could guess the exact amount of rudder needed at the last instant before touchdown. Either too little rudder or too much rudder is going to result in a side load on the main landing gear. You also need to get the nosewheel down early with this procedure (before the airplane has a chance to weathervane as speed dissipates) and hold up-aileron into the wind.

Fig. 3-9. The Goodyear crosswind landing gear took some getting used to. Touchdown and rollout were accomplished while crabbed into the wind.

Nevertheless, the wing-low procedure is the simplest of the two methods and requires no last-second adjustments. Control your airspeed with pitch as usual, and your rate of descent with power, and you'll soon become comfortable with this technique. Drop a wing into the wind as you complete your turn from base to final approach (some pilots initially crab into the wind in order to determine the amount of drift, then switch to the wing-low configuration). The amount of bank needed will depend upon wind velocity. Again, be aware of the maximum allowable crosswind component as listed in the owner's manual.

To compensate for the airplane's tendency to turn into the down wing, opposite rudder is applied to maintain your ground track along the extended centerline of the runway. So, you are in a gentle forward slip all the way down final, and you carry this attitude through a normal flare and touchdown. You will touch down on one wheel, and it is important to "hold what you have"—that is, keep the wing low and maintain a straight track down the runway with whatever rudder it takes to do the job (Fig. 3-10).

Throughout the flare, and into touchdown and the subsequent rollout, the flight controls are going to become progressively softer as they always do with diminishing speed, so you will have to apply more and more control pressure to counter the crosswind. Don't relax aileron pressure to help the other main wheel to settle; it will do so rather quickly on its own if you have properly managed your airspeed. Ground friction on the rolling main exerts all the force necessary to bring down the other main. By the time both mains are rolling, you might have the aileron and rudder against their stops. To take advantage of the nosewheel for steering, you can ease off a slight amount of back pressure on the yoke to get the nosewheel down a little sooner than usual. But make certain the rudder is neutral when the nosewheel touches down, otherwise you'll find

Fig. 3-10. Landing in a left crosswind. Left wing low, you'll touch down on the left main wheel.

yourself making a high-speed turnoff much earlier than you had planned. Don't use brakes until all wheels are rolling.

The rollout, taxi, and systems shut-down must be regarded as part of the landing. The flight is not over until the airplane is secured—tied down, hangared, locked—or consigned to the care of trustworthy service personnel. Turbocharged engines need a four- or five-minute cooldown after landing (include taxi time) before shutdown. Two or three minutes at idle power with any reciprocating engine is good insurance against sticking valves and hairline cylinder-head cracks. Then, turn off the boost pump, pull the mixture control into "idle cutoff," and let the propeller come to a complete stop before turning off the ignition. Finally, turn off all electrics and the master switch.

Combined Method. Many pilots feel uncomfortable flying the wing-low method all the way down final with the turn coordinator's ball out of its cage. Therefore, they fly the crab method down final with the nose of the airplane yawed into the wind while tracking the extended runway centerline. Then, when down to about 100 feet above the surface on short final they go to the wing-low attitude and enter the flare with the nose pointed straight down the runway centerline. Timing the switch from a crab to wing-low and adding opposite rudder is a matter of practice. With practice, you can hold the crab down to 20 or 30 feet—right into the beginning of the flare. Of course, in gusty conditions it's best to make the switch a little sooner.

During any crosswind rollout, hold full up-aileron on the upwind wing, and neutral or slightly forward pressure on the yoke. If you must taxi downwind when exiting the runway, do so with full down elevator.

Your owner's manual will have a graph or table that shows the maximum crosswind component for your machine. Much of the time you will have some headwind component and some crosswind component. For example, a wind that is 45° off the runway centerline will have a crosswind component of about ⅔ of the wind velocity. The other ⅓ will be a headwind component.

You will note that the maximum crosswind component as given in the owner's manual will be less than 20 knots for almost all lightplanes—usually closer to 15 knots. If you don't fudge on that figure you won't need to get the upwind wing down very far when employing the wing-low technique. The biggest problems are caused by gusty conditions and wet or icy runways. Normally, you can handle the gusts with a little extra airspeed. A wet or icy runway, swept by a strong crosswind, is probably best handled with prayer.

At uncontrolled airports you may have only the shape of the wind sock as a clue to wind velocity, and it is not going to show you the difference between a 17- and 24-knot wind. Most wind socks, depending upon length, will be fully inflated in any wind greater than 15 knots. If you fly a precise pattern, your drift correction toward or away from the runway may be another clue, although you know the wind is not likely to be exactly the same 1,000 feet below.

Tailwheel Landings

What about the older (classic) airplanes with the nosewheel under the tail? Are they as tricky to land as the airport lounge lizards claim? Not too many years ago airplanes with tailwheels were said to have "conventional" landing gear and, presumably, you made conventional landings in them. The "three-point" landing was regarded as the mark of the accomplished pilot—that is, power at idle as the mains and tailwheel simultaneously touched—lightly—with the airplane fully stalled.

Actually, it wasn't all that difficult in, say, a three-place Piper Super Cruiser, which had a wing loading under 10 pounds per square foot and a stalling speed of 42 MPH fully loaded, operating from a grass field which allowed you to land and take off directly into the wind each time. It got a bit more difficult as speeds and wing loadings went up and paved runways, rather than wind, dictated landing and takeoff direction.

Until the late 1950s almost everyone learned to fly in tailwheel airplanes, and the first Cessna 150, introduced in 1958, was derisively referred to by some of the old hands as having a "training wheel" or "idiot wheel" under its nose. But the tri-gear prevailed because it is easier to land and therefore results in fewer bent airframes. If all of your flying is in a tri-gear airplane, you need to have a few hours of dual instruction in a tailwheel airplane before soloing it.

On airplanes with tailwheels the center of gravity is behind the main wheels, and therefore you must be careful to maintain a straight track down the runway on rollout or the tail will tend to swing around toward the front in what it known as a "ground loop." The usual result is landing gear and prop damage (if you leave the runway) and, perhaps, a bashed wingtip, although it's possible to go over on your back if you get excited and stomp the brakes. (Fig. 3-11)

I've witnessed several ground loops over the years, perhaps the most interesting performed by a Cessna 195 pilot who did a complete 180 on rollout and came to a stop with his tail where his nose should have been. Then there was the would-be lady "aero" pilot who let a clipped-wing Cub get away from her during rollout. She got on the brakes and the Cub went hopping off into the grass with its tail pointed skyward about 45° and its prop shooting sparks. The airplane came to rest on its nose.

As mentioned above, you can land a tailwheel airplane "three point" in a full stall, or on the main gear, tail high, with or without power. The power wheel landing is certainly preferred for crosswinds. For a wheel

Fig. 3-11. When landing a tailwheel-type airplane, you must maintain a straight track down the runway or the tail will tend to swing around toward the front, causing a "ground loop." Pictured is what happens when you stomp the brakes.

landing, set up a normal approach at normal approach speed—higher than normal speed in gusty and/or crosswind conditions—and hold the airplane level after your flare, just a couple of feet above the runway. Then, a slight power reduction will allow the airplane to settle onto its mains. At this point, go forward slightly on the stick (or yoke) to keep the tail up and prevent the airplane from ballooning back into the air. Don't worry about the prop striking the runway; at touchdown velocity you probably could not force the tail that high with the wheels rolling.

If the wheel landing is made power-off, do it the same way except, instead of reducing power for touchdown, relax your back pressure on the stick a little to let the airplane settle onto the mains and, again, ease in some forward stick to hold the airplane in level attitude until speed dissipates.

When a tailwheel airplane is in a three-point attitude (tail down), the wing tends to cancel some of the airflow over the tail (Fig. 3-12). The situation is compounded during a full stall landing with power at idle and the resulting weak slipstream. Some rudder is desirable to help the tailwheel keep the rollout straight ahead. Three-point an old biplane that has a tailskid in place of a "newfangled" steerable tailwheel, and you'll appreciate the rudder. (I can still hear one of my early instructors, "Stay sharp on the rudder, boy!")

The three-point landing in a "taildragger" (I don't like the term, but you can't avoid it these days) has long been described as stalling the airplane about six inches above the surface, power at idle. The flare is managed so that the stick is back against the stops as the airplane settles on mains and tailwheel simultaneously. No points are subtracted if the tailwheel touches slightly before the main wheels, but if the main gear is solidly down while the tail is still flying, it's probably best to treat it as a power-off wheel landing and complete the landing accordingly.

So what is the secret of consistently good tailwheel landings? The keys are to hold the tail on the ground during rollout, and make prompt corrections to maintain a straight track. A good tailwheel installation, with strong springs and a horizontally mounted swivel plate, is extremely

Fig. 3-12. A three-point, full-stall landing is easier if the wind cooperates. If you learned to fly in a tri-gear, obtain some dual from an experienced tailwheel airplane instructor if you want to fly these machines.

important. Also, taxi these airplanes at a leisurely pace, and with a series of S-turns providing good forward vision.

Brakes are important on a tailwheel airplane because they are
sometimes needed to augment the action of the steerable tailwheel in
a crosswind, and because they can become your only means of steering
on rollout if the tailwheel shimmies and becomes ineffective due to weak
springs, bent control arms, or excessive wear. Don't be heavy-footed and
lock-up the downwind brake; tap lightly, then increase pressure as
needed.

Wet and Icy

Hydroplaning, the development of a film of water between your tires
and the runway surface, may begin at 38-40 knots in lightplanes, depending upon aircraft weight and tire pressure. The type of surface is also
a factor. Asphalt, of course, is highly conductive to this condition while
grooved concrete is not. Hydroplaning is a dangerous situation because
you lack both control and braking efficiency.

When faced with a wet runway, that is, wet enough that hydroplaning
may be a factor, your landing technique will be dictated by wind
conditions. At controlled airports, the ATIS broadcast will include braking
action advisories, and Tower will give them too. If the wind is no more
than 10° off the runway you haven't too much of a problem, even in a
tailwheel airplane. But keep in mind that even this depends upon wind
velocity, because the headwind you land into becomes a crosswind as
you taxi off the runway, and it may be too strong for you to taxi on a
slick surface.

A crosswind landing on a slick surface can be a challenge in a tri-
gear and an adventure in a tailwheel machine, and your options are
limited. In a tri-gear airplane you can limit yourself to a maximum
crosswind component of 50% of normal and employ short-field landing
techniques, or you may insist upon landing into the wind (especially if
you are flying a tailwheel airplane). The latter choice may mean going
to another airport or landing in the grass. Some airports with paved
runways also have designated grass strips. If the airport is controlled,
ask the controller. It's true that wet grass doesn't offer much in the way
of a good braking surface, but it is still an option if you need to eliminate
an unacceptable crosswind. It requires soft-field technique (I'll discuss
soft-field and short-field landings in the following chapter).

Ice and packed snow on the runway constitute the worst landing
situations with any significant crosswind, along with the fewest options
(Fig. 3-13). Common sense will be your principal guide – which means
that, if employed soon enough, you leave your airplane in the hangar.

Fig. 3-13. Flying off skis entails some special techniques and new rules. If you intend to engage in this kind of flying, you'll need a checkout with an instructor experienced in such operations. *(Joseph P. Juptner)*

Most of us have had experience driving our automobiles on ice, and it appears that many of our fellow drivers tend to lose all reason once their drive wheels lose traction. On perfectly level streets they can be seen spinning their wheels at high speed, tires smoking, as they floorboard their accelerator pedals and go nowhere. Meanwhile, drivers with a modicum of self-discipline and common sense, barely touching their accelerators, move gingerly around the wheel-spinners and proceed to their destinations.

The wheels of an airplane have no power. If you must use an icy runway, short-field technique is probably best if the surface is smooth; soft-field technique if the wind has carved humps and ridges. Stay off the brakes.

You can't always judge the condition of a runway by observing it from the air, and the presence of a control tower or Flight Service station is no guarantee that you will be informed of all possible undesirable situations. I remember going into (controlled) Wiley Post Airport at Bethany, Oklahoma, one winter morning when I could see pretty white patterns across the runway that looked like ripples on a pond. I assumed that it was wind-blown snow. It wasn't. It was wind-blown *sleet* that had frozen solid in little ridges three or four inches high. I don't know why I didn't blow a tire or two, or wipe out the Comanche's nose gear. That was a rough rollout.

Crosswind landings are certainly interesting on icy runways, and included in the standard advice for handling such situations is the suggestion that you land on the upwind edge of the runway and trust that you can complete your rollout before drifting off the downwind edge of the runway—or weathervaning and sliding sideways into a snow bank. Fly the standard crosswind approach, and touch down on the upwind main. The other main may need a tiny bit of help due to reduced surface friction. Then get the nosewheel down. Do not use brakes; and because you are using no more than 20% of flaps, just leave them as is. Flap retraction is not going to help much in transferring weight to the wheels more quickly and you don't need another distraction at this point. Use your flight controls to the fullest, because that's all you've got, and expect the rudder to become ineffective below about 30–35 knots.

If you find the above advice inadequate compared to what you had hoped for, then I suggest that you face up to the truth with me: There are some things that you should not try in an airplane until you have years of flying experience. By that time, you'll know better than to try them.

A cleared runway with icy patches is another situation that calls for no brakes. The danger of asymmetrical braking, which would spin the airplane into a sudden ground loop, overrides any benefit you might derive from the use of brakes.

Visibility—or the lack of it—might dictate landing techniques akin to those sometimes employed at night (I'll talk about night landings in the following chapter). Visibility in cold weather can be fabulous away from industrial areas, but there are also those dark and hazy days when recent snowfall makes depth perception difficult, particularly at small uncontrolled airports. Here you can borrow from the floatplane pilot's textbook: Set up a 100-150 FPM rate of descent on final approach and hold it right into touchdown. There is no law that says you have to flare in the ground cushion—airliners never do.

If you are forced to land in mud, slush, snow, or a combination of these, it's best to extend no more than 20–25° of flaps and carry a little extra airspeed onto the runway with the nose high. The drag of the mushy surface on the landing gear will tend to pitch the nose down, and meanwhile the extra airspeed will also help keep the flight controls effective until a straight rollout is established. Land a tailwheel airplane the same way on such a surface.

4

Short, Soft, and Dark

THE FLIGHT PORTION OF THE PRIVATE PILOT EXAMINATION REQUIRES that you demonstrate both short-field and soft-field landing techniques. Both are rather easily mastered. The hard part is staying in practice once you've become proficient at them. Many pilots promptly forget these procedures soon after the flight examiner steps from the airplane. They have never operated from less than a mile of concrete, and they tend to view short-field and soft-field landings as training exercises, like ground reference maneuvers. That attitude usually doesn't last.

Short-Field Approach and Landing

One thing should be said in the beginning about short-field (and soft-field) landings: The fact that you do not intend to use a lot of ground does not necessarily mean that you should fly a tight pattern with an abbreviated final approach. Just the opposite is true, wind and surrounding terrain permitting. When possible, take your time, fly a standard pattern, and give yourself plenty of room on final to set things up as carefully as you can. Extend full flaps as soon as you level out on final approach, and get your airspeed stabilized at no more than 1.3 V_{so}, assuming that you are not also faced with turbulence or gusty wind conditions.

Getting full flaps down early (perhaps before you are certain that you have the field made) is contrary to your usual procedure, but you might be a little higher than normal to clear obstructions just off the runway threshold, and early deployment of full flaps allows more time to stabilize the approach so that the only control change you should need is a touch of power.

If you are too high, do not dive for the runway. Reduce power if you can; otherwise, apply full power and go around for another try.

I once heard short-field landings described as, "like any other landings, except more so." That is a good description. It is important that you select your desired touchdown spot and stick with it. The short-field landing is a precision landing. In actual practice, a number of factors must be taken into account when planning any landing, but *real* short-field landings often include wind conditions and topography that you are normally seldom confronted with.

Wind is always a factor and can be tricky in mountain country. Temperature is important, and heat combined with high altitude means a high *true* airspeed (TAS), although your *indicated* airspeed (IAS) is right where it should be. Where should it be? Your owner's manual may give a lower figure, which is alright in smooth air and no possibility of terrain-induced turbulence, but your regular approach speed of 1.3 times flaps-down power-off stall speed is usually a safe figure for the approach. The indicated airspeed is the one you use, of course, because it is the one your airplane "feels." At any given weight and attitude the plane will always stall at the same IAS regardless of the TAS. If you have trouble picturing the relationship between IAS (where the needle points on your airspeed indicator) and TAS, remember that your airspeed indicator is a pressure instrument; you have to go faster through thin air to make it indicate the same as it would going slower in denser air.

The spot you select for touchdown must allow a safe margin over any obstacles on the approach and provide the maximum possible rollout area beyond touchdown. It's best to make this approach under power, and with a higher-than-usual angle of attack, using pitch to control airspeed. Cut power just before touchdown, and apply brakes as soon as soon as the mains are rolling. Brake smoothly, with increasing pressure; don't stomp the brakes. Keep the yoke all the way back—ideally it should reach the stops just as the mains touch—and retract the flaps as soon as you can to get the weight on the main wheels and increase brake effectiveness.

There is another way to do it, usually referred to as "dragging it in," which gets the airspeed way down, actually below the airplane's normal power-off stall speed. The approach is flown with a high power setting and very high angle of attack. You are literally "hanging on the prop," and when the throttle is cut the airplane quits flying immediately. This is actually an emergency procedure that requires a fine touch; but later, as you gain experience, you should know how to do it in your airplane just in case it ever becomes necessary.

I once saw Larry Ball (author of *Those Incomparable Bonanzas*) demonstrate this procedure in a 260-HP Bonanza V-tail. At the time, Larry was in charge of Bonanza sales at the Beech factory, and I had gone to Wichita for a demo ride. Not many people have more time in V-tails than Larry. He had a new airplane, a cool day, and we were 200 pounds under gross. Still, it was an impressive demonstration.

The two of us flew over to Newton, Kansas, for what Larry characterized as "minimum-field" landings. That's flat country, and there were no obstacles to a low approach. With gear and flaps down, nose high, and under high power, Ball made the approach at 50 MPH IAS, which was 10 MPH below the gear-and-flaps-down-power-off stalling speed listed in the owner's manual. As the runway threshold disappeared under our nose, Larry closed the throttle, the Bonanza was on the pavement immediately, and we stopped in approximately 330 feet. I was able to obtain a fairly close measurement because I left the airplane and determined that the expansion joints in the runway were 21 feet apart. The wind was on our nose at 5-10 MPH. I don't recall the temperature or altimeter setting, but it was a nice demonstration, I thought, and I included it in a little book I did about those airplanes. However, it turned out that Larry thought we were just stooging around, and did not understand that I intended to write about the events of that morning. When he saw it in print, he asked that we add 10 MPH to his approach speed because, he said, an inexperienced pilot, trying to duplicate the procedure in a Bonanza, might get into trouble. After so many years, maybe Larry will forgive me if I tell it like it really was.

Soft-Field Landings

The soft-field landing is accomplished by what I choose to describe as a "modified drag-in." Use approximately 50% power during approach, with full flaps and gear down, maintaining an IAS of $1.3\ V_{so}$ or a little less, and controlling airspeed with pitch as usual. This should allow some flexibility in your descent rate because you can add or subtract a little power as required and achieve good precision in touching down quite close beyond your reference spot.

Now, pay attention; here's how to touch like a feather (Fig. 4-1). As you descend to the height where you normally begin your flare, continue back pressure on the yoke to further erode your airspeed and slowly increase power. Now, you are working on the back side of your power

Fig. 4-1. Cessna Stationair makes a soft-field landing under power and with low airspeed.

curve (some call it the "area of reverse command"), with airspeed below V_{so}, and as long as you continue to apply up-elevator, that additional power is going to result in slower flight.

All of your attention must be outside the airplane; keep it straight with rudder and allow no side drift. If this is an off-airport landing, try to select a prominent terrain feature in the distance to use as your "straight ahead" guide. You do these last few feet by feel alone. The IAS will be without value anyway, because you are at least 5 knots below your normal touchdown speed.

With the nose high and under power, you will very gradually descend to the surface. With a little practice, your wheels will touch ever so lightly. As soon as you are sure you have touched down, you may cut power to the extent desired. Usually, surface conditions and wind will make this decision for you. In soft ground or snow, you might want to keep moving and taxi to a firmer surface. Keep the nosewheel light with up-elevator, and don't use brakes except in an emergency. Many instructors will tell you to get the flaps up to avoid damaging them with rocks, ice, etc. (Fig. 4-2). But if the surface is really soft and the situation argues that you keep moving, it has always seemed to me that it's better to keep the airplane as light on its wheels as possible by taking whatever tiny amount of lift you can get at that speed. A fast taxi is not a good idea on a soft surface. If the main wheels are momentarily slowed by any kind of obstacle, that can cause the nosewheel to burrow into the mush. The pace of a brisk walk is the best taxi speed. The important thing is to keep moving.

As I noted earlier, there are people around who have not practiced short-field or soft-field landings since the U.S. Government certified them as practicing private pilots, but I am privileged to know some very good pilots who seldom land any other way. They do short-field landings on 8,600-foot runways in the flatlands. They clearly put a lot of effort into each landing. It's not just pride—though I'm sure there is some of that involved—but also the fact that it keeps their skills sharply honed for those occasions when such techniques are essential.

Grass Airstrips

Study any Sectional chart, especially those covering areas outside the Northeast air corridor, and you may be surprised at the number of unpaved airport symbols you can find. There may be more places you can land a lightplane on grass than on concrete or asphalt.

Fig. 4-2. An old asphalt runway in the high desert is treated as a soft field because it contains soft spots. In the West and Southwest it pays to ask local pilots about primitive fields.

If you plan to fly into a grass strip that is strange to you, phone ahead to determine field condition, along with anything else the operator or FBO can tell you, *including how to locate it from the air*. If the field is unattended, use extreme caution. A hard rain within the past 48 hours may have left the field too soft for safe operation, although this depends upon the type of soil, drainage, and the amount of sun and wind since the rain. Another problem is that some grass strips in the boonies may remain on Sectionals when they are no longer maintained as landing areas.

The barnstormers of the 1920s used strange grass fields almost exclusively. One such barnstormer, the late Earl Reed (who obtained the first clipped-wing Cub STC) told me that standard procedure was to inspect the pasture selected for operations (it had to be on the edge of town and bordering a road) by making a couple of slow passes at 100 feet to look for obstacles such as gopher holes, rocks, and deep ruts caused by ground vehicles. They also looked for hog feeding troughs not in use, which worked well as wheel chocks. It's unlikely that you will find a handy hog trough, but the rest of Earl's procedure remains valid. Get down low and slow and inspect the unattended field as best you can if you absolutely must land there. In my view, it's better to fly a little farther, land where conditions are known, and make up the difference in rented wheels.

Operating from a grass airport, whether your home field or a strange one, your concerns are what common sense tells you they should be: Is the ground soft from recent rain or thaw? Does the grass hide ruts, holes, rocks, or other obstacles? Are there high tension wires bordering the field, and are they marked with orange balls? Is there a phone?

As for flight operations, use soft-field technique. Taxi slowly, and don't expect good braking in wet grass. If you are flying a tri-gear machine, hold the nose off as long as you can when landing, and take off tail-low, the idea being to give your nosewheel every break you can. Grass, depending upon its height, can add up to 50% to a normal takeoff roll. Therefore, it is sometimes desirable to help the airplane to fly off at minimum airspeed and then hold it level in ground effect until you have accelerated to your climb speed, best rate (V_y) or best angle (V_x) as the environment dictates.

If you regularly operate from a grass field, check the air intake (carburetor) filter often, and include a careful inspection of the wheel brake assemblies in each preflight inspection. Keep them free of mud and debris. Tailwheel assemblies also gather a lot of weeds and mud. Pilots who are based on grass fields sometimes re-route hydraulic brake lines to the rear edges of exposed gear legs. They also tape the leading edge of the horizontal stabilizer.

In the Mountains

In the western U.S. there are a lot of airports above 5,000 feet elevation. A few are major terminals; most serve smaller communities. In the mountains, runways are sometimes short, occasionally unpaved, and the winds seemingly unpredictable. Surface winds in the mountains are seldom steady, which means higher landing speeds to compensate fore gusts. The increased airspeed, plus increased ground speed (due to the thinner air—higher density altitude), translate into significantly higher touchdown speeds.

Most airports in the high country are located so that you can—and are expected to—fly a normal traffic pattern. At uncontrolled fields, announce your position and intentions on the published CTAF frequency five miles out, and again just prior to each turn in the pattern. Make every effort to determine surface wind conditions, overflying the strip above pattern altitude, if necessary. Lacking a response from UNICOM, you'll have to use an altimeter setting from the nearest Flight Service Station (FSS). The surrounding terrain might dictate that you fly the final approach a bit high, and in gusty conditions your best approach speed should typically be the same as your best rate-of-climb speed, with 20–25° of flaps deployed. If you have to abort the landing and go around for another approach, you will appreciate the extra airspeed and the fact that you are not carrying full flaps, but the prime reason for this configuration is to have adequate control through the touchdown and rollout.

Retract flaps immediately after touchdown. On hard surfaces with uncooperative winds, get the nosewheel down early. Be aware that, in thin air (high density altitude) your flare prior to touchdown will not check your rate of descent as it does in denser air, and be prepared to soften your landing with a touch of power.

It is important to determine which way, if any, the airstrip slopes. Uphill runways can trick you into believing that you are higher than you are, while a landing area or runway that slopes downhill can make you think you are lower than you actually are. Sloping runways also do not allow the use of a fixed reference with which to judge your touchdown point.

Except for the capricious winds and the lack of weathercasts, the greatest concern for the average lightplane pilot in mountain flying is dealing with the question of density altitude. You will recall from ground school classes that pressure altitude is your indicated altitude with the altimeter set at 29.92 Hg. Corrected for temperature, it is density altitude, which is the altitude in which your airplane "thinks" it is operating, regardless of its actual height above either sea level or the terrain below.

The density altitude of an airport located at 5,000 feet elevation can easily be 6,000 feet or more at noon on a warm day—higher if a low pressure air mass covers the area. If you refer to the takeoff chart in the airplane's owner's manual, you will note that you start with your gross weight and find the required takeoff run and the distance for a takeoff over a 50-foot obstacle after including wind, altitude, and temperature. There may be a small fudge factor included, but I think it's wise to add another 5-10% for aircraft age and less-than-perfect pilot technique.

In mountain country dependable weathercasts are rare. Weather reporting stations are spread thinly over the western states, and mountains make their own mini-weather systems. Light zephyrs squeezing through mountain passes from the west can come roaring out the eastern side at 50 knots. Orographic thunderstorms develop when a relatively moist air mass (usually off the Pacific) is pushed up the western slopes of the mountains by the prevailing westerlies until it reaches its dew point. Convective thunderstorms also form over the mountains on summer afternoons.

In the valleys, the mountains' leeward slopes are generally to be avoided. The wind spilling over the summit rolls down toward the valley floor, affected by terrain irregularities. Surface friction does tend to slow the air mass, but it also causes turbulence.

Wind shear is common in the mountains, and can occur vertically as well as horizontally. It can be the result of a microburst from the bottom of a mature thunderhead or other convective activity, or it can be caused by a warm air mass flowing across a mass of cooler air trapped in a valley. There is surprisingly little mixing together of two dissimilar air masses when they come together, and there will always be a turbulent transition zone along the boundaries.

Night Landings

Sometimes, walking through the pilots' lounge, you can hear some interesting statements. For example: "If you go flying at night in a single-engine airplane, you start out with an emergency." But you know how pilots are. They either overstate or understate to get a point across. Lots of people routinely fly single-engine airplanes on night cross-countries and think nothing of it.

I know one pilot who flies his Cessna Cardinal on night cross-countries between lighted airports that are no more than 30 miles apart. He reasons that, in the event of engine failure, from a cruising altitude of at least 10,000 feet he can almost certainly glide 15 miles to the nearest landing patch. I suppose that works alright in the eastern part of the U.S., but west of the Mississippi, airports are fewer and farther between. There, some of us tend to follow the interstates at low altitudes, secure in the belief that we have an emergency landing strip just below throughout the flight. The rest of us seek no painless sops to our fears, believing that the best insurance against a forced landing is good preflight planning and a properly maintained airplane, along with the judgment to fly or not to fly based upon the capability of our machines and ourselves for each situation.

Personally, I regard the light twins (180 HP on each side) with 4,000-foot single-engine ceilings as far more risky at night than a single-engine airplane—which has a single-engine service ceiling three times higher. That 4,000-foot ceiling soon dwindles to zero over the Alleghenies or west of Amarillo. Over more than half of the country there's no margin for a hot summer night or a little dab of ice on the wings.

Admittedly, that's no way to justify a decision to fly single-engine at night. You do it because you weigh the risk against the need—and then hold your thumb on the faith side of the scale. It's a personal decision.

Approaching controlled airports at night, you will be told when and how to enter the traffic pattern. At uncontrolled fields, always fly a standard pattern, transmitting your position and intentions on the appropriate CTAF. Because it is often difficult to judge your height above the surface as you near the runway, and accurate altimeter setting is important, and you need to know airport elevation, along with direction and velocity. It's often difficult enough to find a wind indicator on a strange airport in daytime, but at night it can be even worse. You might have to overfly the field looking for it.

Some instructors advise flying a steep approach at night, but it seems to me that a normal approach, carrying enough power so that you have the flexibility to shorten or lengthen the final as necessary, is the surest way. Use 20–25° of flaps.

If you should find yourself following a "heavy" on final approach, plan your touchdown at least half way down the runway in order to avoid his dangerous wake turbulence. At night, you'll find it very difficult to tell just where the big jet actually touches down, which is where those twin tornadoes spiraling off his wingtips cease. You can usually assume that he will be on the concrete before using up half of it. The remaining half should be plenty for you. In all cases, maintain the proper spacing between your airplane and the one ahead, particularly if it is a big one. The controller is supposed to do this, and he/she is supposed to do it with regard to wake turbulence, but some towers are closed during the wee hours, although airline and military traffic may continue.

The problem with night landings is that of judging distance, or depth perception. Your personal "depth perceptor" works just as well at night, but the clues it gets are too few and too inconsistent too often. For example, because a runway can have any width, the distance between the left and right rows of runway lights is not standard. A night landing at an unfamiliar airport can therefore be interesting, even on the clearest of nights. You can look straight down the runway from short final and be thoroughly confused. Wide spacing between the rows of lights can give you the impression that you are higher than normal, while rows that are closer together than you have been accustomed to can make you seem low. VASIs have aided a great deal in this respect, especially if you have resisted the temptation to habitually expand on their directions. Approach light systems can also help give you some perspective of runway dimensions.

I won't try to explain all of that rod and cone business about the human eyeball because I don't remember much of it and doubt if you care that much anyway. It's probably enough to say that you have a blind spot in the focal center of your eye at night that covers about 5°, and that is why your vision improves when you direct your eyes 10° or so from the object to be seen.

"Stare vision" is one of the tricks your eyes can play at night, when a fixed or stationary light appears to move in wide arcs. If the light is moving, it may seem to move to one side while in reality it is moving straight ahead. So, don't stare; keep shifting from one point to another.

One of the most significant results of an Air Force study of night vision problems was that people who normally spend 2–5 hours in bright sunshine in the afternoon require up to 5 hours to adapt to darkness. That is why you should wear sunglasses. Air Force specifications are for sunglasses that admit no more than 15% of bright sunlight. A specialist in pilots' visual problems, optometrist Warren DeHaan of Boulder, Colorado (who holds an airline transport pilot certificate) recommends lens of reddish-brown or gray tint.

Night flight has its compensations. The air is generally smoother, controllers aren't as busy, and since strobe lights have become common on airplanes, other aircraft are much easier to see, that is, if they are at your level or above. Airplanes below and over a city—where they may be approaching the same uncontrolled airport you intend as a destination—tend to blend into the mass of lights below.

Once the runway is made, reduce power, continue down, and begin your flare at what you perceive to be approximately a wingspan above the surface. As you flare, bring in enough power to hold the airplane in landing attitude above the runway. Then, a slight power reduction will allow the airplane to gently settle until the main wheels begin to roll.

What's that? Soft-field technique, you say? You've got it.

Once on the ground at a strange airport, there is often a bewildering array of lights in all directions to intimidate you. The controller will always direct you off the runway onto a blue-lighted taxiway, but if he is busy he might appear to lose interest in you at that point. At large airports, he will hand you over to Ground Control, and that controller will direct you to wherever you want to go on the airport. If you don't receive these directions, ask for them, using the radio frequency of your last contact. Do not switch from tower frequency until told to do so.

After your turn off onto a taxiway, keep your landing (or taxi) light on. There is no telling what you might encounter on a taxiway.

It must be recognized that there is more than one kind of night flight. There is the kind that you can fly soon after sunset, just before sunrise, on one of those clear nights with a full moon, and on nice evenings when the profusion of surface lights provide a definite horizon and other visual references. You can limit your night flying to such conditions and log the required landings to satisfy the currency provisions of your pilot's certificate. But that kind of night flying does not prepare you for cross-country VFR for any appreciable distance. Sometimes, it can get pretty dark out there.

Not long ago, a pilot and his wife died across town from where I write this. He was an automobile dealer from a town in northern Oklahoma. He and his wife had spent the evening with friends here, then took off to fly home shortly before midnight. He filed Special VFR because of a thin layer of fog that had begun to form during the previous hour. As he took off, he almost immediately began a climbing turn to the left and continued around a great arc until impact a mile from the airport.

About a year later, I lost a longtime friend in an almost identical situation, except that he took off shortly before sunrise and filed no flight plan. There was a light fog, later reported as 1/16 mile. He was airborne about two minutes. Three companions died with him.

Both of these tragedies could have easily been avoided. All these pilots had to do (short of delaying takeoff) was set their directional gyros to conform with the runway heading prior to takeoff and then hold that heading during climbout.

This brings up the proposition that a growing number of pilots are endorsing: All night cross-country should be IFR. I have come to support this position despite my proclivity to resist any federal regulation that isn't absolutely necessary to the sun coming up tomorrow. However, I can tell you that you aren't likely to fly night cross-country VFR for very long before you find yourself in IFR conditions. It's a little unsettling to be sailing along on a clear night, all the needles obedient to your wishes, and suddenly note a rosy glow around your wingtip as your navigation light reflects the presence of cloud.

In fact, you can become totally disoriented at night when there is no impediment to visibility. I remember such an occasion. The late Chuck

Wolfe and I left Mercedes, Texas—way down at the southern tip of Texas on the Mexican border—in a Bellanca Viking about 9:00 P.M. and climbed into a moonless but unlimited sky that was absolutely crowded with stars. Now, I've never been on the ground down there, but I'm sure there is nothing but sandhills and coyotes, maybe a ranch house here and there. On a moonless night from 9,500 feet the surface is solid black, punctuated by an occasional, tiny light.

As we progressed toward San Antonio, I found it increasingly difficult to tell where the horizon should be. Then I had the feeling that we were climbing steeply. I could not distinguish between the stars and the lights on the ground. The attitude gyro showed straight and level. I looked at Chuck in the dim light of the instruments and saw that he was looking at me. I'm sure that he read the situation perfectly (he was an old Navy pilot). He motioned to the glow of a city in the distance off the right wing. "We can get some great seafood over at Corpus Christi," he said.

I banked toward the patch of light, concentrating on the attitude indicator. "You want to take it?" I asked/suggested.

I felt slightly dizzy, and I was angry with myself. I should have filed IFR. I should have gone on autopilot. I should have had more sense.

Chuck dialed in the new heading and engaged the autopilot. The seafood was indeed great.

My point is that vertigo is an insidious thing. It can happen to anyone under a variety of conditions—even on a perfectly clear night.

One other observation about night flight from personal experience: My night vision improved dramatically after I stopped smoking. I hate to agree with all those meddling do-gooders who make such an issue of it, but I've got to tell it like it is.

5

Takeoffs

"WHAT'S TO KNOW ABOUT TAKEOFFS?" DAUGHTER SANDRA ASKED. "I'VE watched. All you have to do is give it the gas and steer, right?"

She was only 12 years old at the time so I didn't take her assessment too seriously. "It takes a lot of body English," I said, silently resolving to volunteer no more words of aeronautical wisdom to my blase girl-type child until she had accumulated a few more years.

Actually, there is quite a lot to know about takeoffs, depending upon where you start. Every takeoff, whether for a cross-country flight or a local pleasure hop, must be preceded by a certain amount of planning and checking. The go/no-go decision properly begins and ends with weather considerations, but there are a host of other factors, also critical to a safe flight, including such things as a preflight inspection of the airplane, a check of its operating systems, and the determination that the pilot is not only qualified by training and experience for the task at hand, but physically fit as well.

Fatigue may be the most common of the physically debilitating threats. To be a pilot is to be a decision maker. Every time you fly you must make a number of decisions, many of which cannot be delayed, most of which are irrevocable, and some of which ensure your continued good health. Fatigue dilutes the quality of your decisions, and it must be a consideration in your preflight planning, especially at night. (The FAA recommends supplemental oxygen above 5,000 ft at night.)

Let us assume now that the go/no-go decision has come up "go," that the flight plan has been filed, and you are leaving the pilots' lounge to walk to the airplane. Acquire the habit of looking at the airplane as you approach it, so that a low shock strut, area of wrinkled skin, or other abnormality is noted (Fig. 5-1). Also, watch for things lying around such as tool boxes, step ladders, and fueling equipment that could be a hazard when taxiing. If your airplane is tied down on an airport where there are several rows of lightplanes, always assume, while moving among them, that *every* propeller is either rotating or will begin rotating at any instant.

Hand Propping

I'm sure that you have an effective routine for the preflight inspection ("walk around") of your aircraft, so I won't give a detailed account of mine except to mention a few procedures that you may not have encountered so far and which may prove useful someday.

Sooner or later you are going to be asked by a pilot to "swing my

Fig. 5-1. Acquire the habit of looking at the airplane as you approach it, so that a low shock strut, area of wrinkled skin (especially around landing gear attach areas), or other abnormalities are noted.

prop.'' His battery is dead and he wants his engine cranked by the "Armstrong" method. If his airplane is a tri-gear, offer to get in the cockpit and handle the switch while *he* swings the propeller. Tell him that his insurance is probably invalid in case of accident with an "unqualified" party propping the airplane. Besides, there *is* a risk involved—you may be surprised at how many serious injuries and fatalities result from propeller accidents each year, with pilots at the top of the list—therefore, it's only proper that the party needing the help either assume the risk himself or have his battery removed and charged.

The risk in hand-propping an airplane is greater with tri-gear machines because of the low thrust line of their engines. When you swing a propeller on a tri-gear, you tend to lunge *into* the prop as you follow-through. It's not as bad on tailwheel airplanes because the prop is at eye level or above and it's easy to step backwards as part of your follow-through motion. If the prop kicks back, it can't bash you.

If the dead battery happens to be in *your* airplane, the proper solution is to have it removed and charged. In cold weather, you can get a jump-start from your automobile if your airplane has a 12-volt system; but this procedure usually doesn't provide enough voltage through your voltage regulator to get your alternator on line (you don't have this problem with the old-style generator system).

If your situation requires a hand start, make sure that you have a pilot or licensed aircraft mechanic at the controls with the parking brake set. Wheel chocks are recommended if they have generous lengths of rope attached so they can be removed from behind the engine. It's best to leave the tail tiedown in place. If you must stand on ice, wet grass, or loose gravel in order to swing the prop, move the airplane. Good footing is absolutely necessary. Also make sure that your prop blast is directed so that it cannot cause damage to other aircraft, cars, etc.

To begin this starting procedure, make sure that the ignition switch is in the OFF position. Then, facing the propeller, rotate it counterclockwise to position the blade on your left a little above horizontal. Stand close enough to obtain a good hold on the blade, but with *only the tips* of your fingers over the upper edge of the blade. Leaning forward in an unbalanced stance can cause you to fall into the blade as the engine starts.

In the airplane, with the throttle set to the normal start position (about ¼ to ½-inch open on our Cessna 150), the ignition (magneto) switch is turned to the BOTH position, and then you pull the blade down rapidly. The best way to ensure that there is no misunderstanding between you and the helper in the airplane is to employ the terms and sequence that were standard back in the days before most airplanes had electric starters:

Hand propper: "Switch Off!" He stands clear and awaits reply.

Pilot in Cockpit: "Switch off!" He must physically touch the switch and confirm that it is off.

The hand propper then positions the prop for the starting attempt:

Hand propper: "Contact!"

Pilot in Cockpit: Turns ignition switch to BOTH position and responds, "Contact!"

Hand propper: Pulls the blade through to start the engine. If the engine does not start, he does *not* return to reposition the propeller for another try until calling, "Switch off!" and receiving that echo from the cockpit.

The procedure is simple, repetitive, and effective. Its purpose is to protect the hand propper.

If the airplane has a propeller spinner, keep in mind while hand propping that the spinner might be used to catch yourself with one hand should you lose your footing and fall toward the propeller as the engine starts.

The spinner is often neglected in the preflight inspection, but it should be checked for security of attachment. Spinners have come off in flight. If there are invisible cracks radiating from the spinner's attach bolts, you probably can feel them by grasping the spinner in both hands and attempting to work it in an eccentric circle.

And while on this subject, I'd like to stress the importance of checking the propeller for those textbook "nicks, dents, and scratches." The outer third of your propeller blades do almost all the work, so pay particular attention there. Any deep scratch in that area should be called to the attention of your mechanic. It could provide a stress point that could lead to blade failure in flight (Fig. 5-2). You should know that when a prop blade departs the airplane in flight, the vibration is so instant and severe that you will be able to turn off the ignition only with the greatest difficulty before the engine shakes itself free of its mounts—after which, the airplane will be so out of balance it *cannot* be controlled. Some years ago at Ft. Worth, I saw a propeller blade fail in flight on aerobatic champ Hal Krier's Chipmunk. Krier was inverted at about 200 feet (how's *that* for an emergency?), and the Ranger engine wrenched from its mounts within three or four seconds. Meanwhile, Krier rolled upright and put the Chipmunk on the ground in a left forward slip with the engine hanging between the main wheels, attached to the airplane by its fuel and oil lines (teflon, covered with braided steel wire). Krier agreed that he was lucky;

Fig. 5-2. The leading edge of this propeller blade has been substantially filed to smooth out stone damage. This owner is crowding the allowable maximum for such a fix.

strong as they were, those fluid lines certainly would not have held the engine for long.

Cockpit Management

Let's assume that you checked the weight-and-balance data and that baggage is stowed within limits as to max weight and CG. It's not much of a problem with a side-by-side trainer, but you must acquire the habit of checking your load and its placement within the aircraft. Also, always determine that outside baggage doors are secure before entering the airplane.

You will take aboard the airplane with you the aeronautical charts appropriate to the planned flight, along with notepad and pencil, as well as your air navigation pocket computer, either the old standby E6B-type circular slide rule or one of the neat new microchip kind. Check the cabin for loose articles that might be tossed about in turbulent air.

There is one other item you should take along that has nothing to do with flying or navigating the airplane, but much to do with a future pleasure: Place your 35mm camera, loaded with film for color prints, in a map pocket, glove compartment, or other handy place where it can't be tossed about. Don't complicate things with extra lenses or other gadgets (maybe a yellow filter if you want to shoot clouds). And don't rest the camera on any part of the airframe for inflight photos; the vibration will blur the results. Much of your shooting will be on the ground: the people you fly with, fellow pilots, etc. Twenty years from now, you will thank me for this suggestion.

I hope you have, and use, printed pre-start and pre-takeoff checklists—yes, even in a two-place trainer. Read each item aloud and then physically touch or appropriately adjust that switch or control.

The Primer

Now, about your primer. You should have an accurate mental picture of what goes on inside your airplane's operating systems if you expect to correctly employ them, and this device is one that many pilots do not really understand. Your primer is an atomizer. Its purpose is to inject atomized gasoline into the engine's fuel induction system. In carbureted recips, the primer should be needed only for cold engine starts. Pull it out slowly to fill it with gasoline, then push it in quickly to obtain the best atomization of the raw fuel. Liquid gasoline in your combustion chambers will not ignite; only the gasoline/air mixture will burn. A cold airplane engine does not need a *richer* mixture in order to start, it needs a mixture that will *ignite*.

The reason that your motor car starts when your airplane won't is mostly due to the unique design of the fuel induction system on the lightplane's opposed, air-cooled engine. In most lightplanes the primer nozzle discharges into the intake manifold which is routed through the oil sump and then upward through risers to each cylinder. In other words, the fuel/air mixture has a long way to go before it reaches the combustion chamber it is destined for. When the oil is cold there is not much fuel vapor left by the time it reaches the cylinders because fuel vaporization is a function of temperature. When the oil is hot it heats the fuel/air mix being drawn through the oil sump and that aids vaporization. That is one reason why external oil preheaters are useful in cold weather. The other reason is that warm oil is ready to flow through the engine's lubricating system immediately upon engine start. Start your engine with cold oil and you have bare metal working against bare metal inside your engine for long seconds before any lubricant film is established, and that subtracts many hours from engine life.

Another primer system found on earlier Continentals is connected directly to the two rear cylinders. It does not work very well. Later versions connect the primer to each cylinder, and this is very effective if you shove the primer handle in hard and obtain good atomization.

There are two time-proven ways to get your airplane started on cold mornings (or following an extended period of inactivity). If your machine has a key start, leave the ignition in the OFF position while you pull the propeller through by hand and a competent helper simultaneously gives it a shot of primer (remember, pull out the primer handle slowly; shove it it hard). This will preload the cylinders with fuel. Then stand clear of the prop as your helper employs the key start. Depending upon temperature and the degree of vaporization achieved, the engine should start with one to three preloads; more will usually flood it.

If you are flying an airplane with a starter button separate from the ignition switch, you can pre-load the cylinders with vaporized fuel without the need for a helper. Crank and prime with the ignition switch in the OFF position. Then effect a normal start. Clearly, the trick is to judge the proper amount of primer use.

On fuel-injected engines, regard the electric auxiliary fuel pump as a primer. Hot starts seem to cause the most trouble for pilots of these planes. The usual advice is that, if all else fails, try following the directions in your owner's manual. Other suggestions include an extended coffee break, allowing time for your winged steed to cool, and pouring cold water on the fuel distributor block to condense what is, after all, a simple old-fashioned vapor lock (and the cold water procedure worked well years ago on our '52 Dodge). The cool-down solution is probably the surest—if you haven't exhausted your battery by the time you decide on it. Progress exacts its price.

Taxiing

If you spend much time around an airport, you will arrive at the conclusion that a lot of lightplanes are unnecessarily damaged while moving on the ground. As previously noted, most landing accidents happen on the landing rollout, apparently because pilots tend to consider a flight completed upon touchdown, and begin to turn their attention to other things. Taxiing, before and after a flight, accounts for more careless-type accidents (Fig. 5-3). Not long ago, I watched helplessly as a pilot taxied his Cherokee toward the parking area, smiling and waving at friends waiting on the apron, and struck the tail of another airplane with his wingtip. As with most taxiing accidents, no one was hurt, but it was expensive. So, the first rule for taxiing an airplane is: Pay attention!

Common sense dictates safe taxi speeds. Some instructors tell their students that taxi speed should not exceed that of a fast walk. The pri-

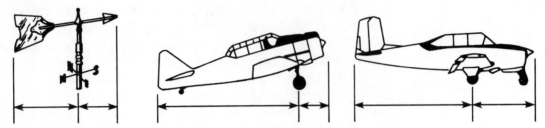

Fig. 5-3. The weathervaning tendency: Because a greater portion of the airplane's surface is presented to a crosswind aft of the main wheels than is presented forward of them, the airplane tends to "weathervane" into any crosswind. The tendency is markedly stronger in tailwheel machines.

mary requirement is positive control; the ability to stop and turn as desired. Turns should be made slowly, but always turn with the airplane moving if possible; pivoting around a locked brake is hard on tires. Maintenance-saving habits indirectly contribute to safety and will directly contribute to your pocketbook when you own your own airplane. Fast turns while taxiing impose a strong side-force on the landing gear, and such turns also can set up an uncontrollable swerve that ends in a damaging ground loop. This is especially true as your airplane goes crosswind when turning from downwind to upwind because of its weathervaning tendency (Fig. 5-4).

Your rudder pedals are your primary directional controls while taxiing. Taxi with your heels on the floor and the balls of your feet low on the rudder pedals. Later, you can rest the arches of your feet on the rudder pedals and toes near the brakes, a position required for simultaneous pressure on the rudder and brake when needed. You will sometimes find it handy to use differential braking to aid in maintaining a straight track in a crosswind landing rollout or during taxi on an icy surface. You can get a little help from your flight controls when taxiing in significant wind. In a crosswind use full up-aileron into the wind. Some pilots will argue that your flight controls are ineffective at speeds below 30-35 knots, and of course you have no business operating a lightplane in a crosswind component of 30 knots or more. That's correct. However, sometimes terrain- or obstacle-induced turbulence or gusts are present, or the crosswind component stronger than anticipated. When judging your personal wind limit, your major concerns are the crosswind and tailwind you have to contend with while taxiing. Taking off into a 20-knot headwind is no problem, but getting to the takeoff position may be.

Normal Takeoff

I hope you don't become weary of my repeated mention of your aircraft owner's manual. It's important that you reference it for a number

Fig. 5-4. The apron at Hilltop Airport is 100 yards wide and 200 yards long. With only three other lightplanes in all that space, the pilot of this Cherokee managed to taxi into one of them. The first rule of taxiing an airplane is, Pay Attention!

of things, including your liftoff and climb speeds under varying conditions. That is where you obtain the base numbers with which to establish the amount of takeoff run you will need at various altitudes, temperatures, and aircraft weights. You have to add your own fudge factors for runway slope and conditions, plus another 10% for the wife and kids. It won't always be exact, but it's a lot better than the grit-yer-teeth-and-hope method.

Most of the data are directly applicable without interpolation. It's true that the book figures were established with a new airplane flown by a professional test pilot, but those performance figures are for max gross weight and while the manufacturer has a little cushion in those recommended figures, time takes its toll on aircraft performance so that, on balance, it's still a good idea to add that extra 10% to all estimated takeoff requirements.

Having taxied into position on the taxiway just short of the runway (behind the double line), perform the pre-takeoff check, reading aloud each item on the printed list (the checklists are sometimes mounted on the instrument panel) and replying aloud as you touch or adjust that control. For example, "Carburetor heat." Touch the knob, look at its position, and reply, "Cold," etc.

You may have set your altimeter to local conditions before you started to taxi if you caught the ATIS broadcast, or Tower (or Ground Control at large airports) will supply the altimeter setting, along with wind, temperature, and taxi instructions. If flying from an uncontrolled airport, the field elevation will be painted on a Burma Shave type sign beside the taxiway. If it's not visible, you can always take it from your Sectional chart.

I'll not detail the pre-takeoff checks except to mention that you should swing the airplane in a complete circle to get an unobstructed view of the entire traffic pattern at uncontrolled airports. Also at uncontrolled fields, you will be transmitting your position and intentions on the CTAF and, of course, monitoring that frequency for the transmissions of other responsible citizens.

Set your directional gyro (DG) to conform with the runway's magnetic bearing. If you don't have an operating DG, you'll have to do it the old-fashioned way—select distant references that you can use in maintaining a straight track during your takeoff run and initial climbout (Fig. 5-5). Usually, of course, you have the runway centerline for takeoff reference.

Fig. 5-5. This is what your instructor means when he says track straight out along the extended runway centerline. That is the runway back there, almost hidden by your rudder.

On grass you will have to use trees, mountains, smokestacks, or something else.

There is no valid reason to take off using less than full power. The air-cooled lightplane engine is designed to operate at full throttle (unless otherwise placarded). As long as the needles of your engine gauges remain in their green arcs, your engine is not being overworked.

Save your concern for a component that needs to be babied a little—the odd wheel of your landing gear, for example. Whether under the nose or under the tail, it is the third wheel on lightplanes that is the most bothersome, both in maintenance and in operation. On takeoff in a tri-gear, unless you have a crosswind to contend with, most instructors will tell you to hold no more forward pressure on the control wheel than is necessary for positive steering. This may mean no forward pressure at all. The key is proper trim. Then you can usually allow the elevators to trail naturally in the slipstream, the object being to lighten the nosewheel as soon as is practicable while still maintaining the airplane in a minimum drag configuration for efficient acceleration. Except in extreme circumstances, avoid the use of differential braking on takeoff because that can throw you into an uncontrollable swerve. It also, of course, prolongs the takeoff roll.

Your best takeoff attitude is close to your airplane's best rate-of-climb attitude. It takes only a small amount of back pressure on the control wheel. You can do this by feel better than by the numbers, which is why you normally establish a liftoff attitude and let the airplane fly itself off. There are exceptions; some airplanes simply have to be lifted off. You'll do them by feel also. The actual airspeed will usually be at least 10% over stalling speed in that configuration and weight, but this can vary; a number of factors can influence your procedure, including runway condition, slope, density altitude, and turbulence.

Crosswind Takeoff

The crosswind takeoff differs from a normal takeoff in two distinct ways: You will hold aileron into the wind, and you should add five knots to your liftoff speed. At the beginning of the takeoff run full up-aileron into the wind is not going to have much effect. The ailerons are the last flight controls to become effective because they are outside the propeller slipstream. Maintain a straight track with rudder as always. However, you may have to hold *downwind* rudder pressure because, on the ground, the airplane (especially tailwheel airplanes) will tend to weathervane. A crosswind from the right may be sufficient to counteract torque (which yaws the airplane to the left), but a wind from the left will aggravate the airplane's left-turning tendency at full power. Use whatever rudder is called for to maintain a straight track down the centerline. The amount of aileron needed will gradually diminish as the ailerons become more effective with increasing speed (Fig. 5-6).

You want that extra five knots at liftoff because you leave the ground in an instant slip into the wind, and you don't want to take a chance that a gust or turbulence will put you back on the ground, however briefly, moving sideways. You may hold your slip into the wind during initial climb, or you can establish a crab with wings level and re-trim after your climbout is set up.

Short-Field Takeoff

The owner's manuals for some airplanes recommend up to 25° of flaps for short-field takeoffs. The owner's manual for our Cessna trainer recommends no flaps. In any case, this is a maximum performance takeoff (Fig. 5-7), and in a fixed-gear trainer the main difference between a short-field takeoff and a normal takeoff is liftoff and initial climb at best-angle-of-climb airspeed, V_x. Once clear of all obstacles, change to best-rate-of-climb speed, V_y. Here is where your slow flight practice helps justify the effort you invested in it. V_x leaves you with little margin for error and requires careful airspeed control.

Takeoff from a short field requires that you use all of the field that is available, and that you accelerate as fast as you can. Years ago, the

Fig. 5-6. As your nosewheel lifts off, your aileron into the slight crosswind may result in your downward wing rising and the downwind main wheel leaving the runway first.

Fig. 5-7. Short-field takeoff in a Debonair with 10° of flaps is demonstrated by Beechcraft expert Larry Ball. He held the brakes as the engine was run up to full thrust to begin the takeoff run. I am along for the ride.

recommended procedure was to hold brakes (or lacking brakes, have helpers hold the wings) while the throttle was opened to maximum. When the RPM reached peak, brakes were released. But when tests showed that this method didn't seem to shorten the takeoff run appreciably, pilots were told to release the brakes and smoothly open the throttle as for a normal takeoff. Now it's back to hold the brakes while you call on the engine for max power, the explanation being that you need to check the mags while the engine is going full bore to make certain that you are going to have maximum power when the brakes are released.

Clearly, you will achieve maximum acceleration by the common sense procedure of presenting the least possible resistance to the air-meaning that you will hold the flight controls in neutral and roll with zero angle of attack—and, if you have any choice, use the ground that offers the least impediment to your wheels. Too often, the short field is also a soft and/or rough field. As a general rule, flap settings of 30° or less produce more lift than drag, but the use of flaps on takeoff also subtracts from acceleration. To get something, you have to give something. While you are told to use no flaps for a short-field takeoff in the Cessna trainer, the owner's manual for the Piper Cherokee says to use 'em.

In tailwheel airplanes, you want to get the tailwheel off the ground and the aircraft in level attitude for maximum acceleration during the takeoff roll. Some instructors recommend a tail-low attitude for tailwheel airplanes during the short-field takeoff run because, they say, that allows the airplane to fly off as soon as it is ready, which is obviously true. The question is, which procedure gets you off the ground quicker with good control? Certainly the latter technique may be dictated for a tri-gear airplane if the short field is also soft, so that your short-field technique becomes more of a soft-field technique. In other words, the short-field takeoff procedure puts emphasis on acceleration, while the soft-field procedure emphasizes getting airborne quickly. There is a difference because you can get off the ground at an airspeed that is insufficient to take you out of ground effect.

Soft-Field Takeoff

Takeoff from a soft field—mud, sand, snow, tall grass, or any surface that retards the takeoff run—is primarily a question of attaining liftoff as quickly as possible, while seeking every ounce of lift you can muster from the instant your wheels begin to roll. Your elevators are in the propeller slipstream and working in slightly compressed air due to their proximity to the surface (unless you are stuck with a stupid T-tail) and are the first flight controls to become effective, allowing you to assume a positive angle of attack soon after you begin to roll. Your immediate objective is to get your nosewheel out of the mush. The nose-high attitude—not too high, about the same as your normal liftoff attitude—will result in a progressive transfer of weight from the mains to the wings as you accelerate.

Theoretically, your slightly nose-high attitude increases drag (remember, drag is a by-product of lift) and subtracts from your acceleration, but lift is your first concern, and you'll accept it at whatever speed gets a few inches of daylight between your mains and the surface. Level off in ground effect, being careful not to push the wheels back into the slush or whatever, and then accelerate—to V_x if there are obstacles to be cleared, to V_y if practicable.

Someone is certain to advise you to get a "running start" if a little bit of firm surface is available, but that can be risky because even a fast taxi speed from a smooth hard surface to a rough soft one will most likely cause your nosewheel to dig itself a hole, whether it is off the ground or not.

The situation can be equally risky if you try to make a high-speed *turn* into the takeoff area after accelerating from a more desirable surface. That may place an unacceptable side load on your landing gear, and it can, if your fuel cell in use is less than half full and not well-baffled inside, force fuel away from the pick-up in the cell, resulting in momentary fuel starvation at a most inopportune time.

Thin Air

High-altitude takeoffs require more *true* airspeed than you are likely to suspect if all your flying has been from fields below, say, 1,500 feet MSL. When density altitude is near 11,000 feet—which is not too unusual at Santa Fe or Albuquerque on a summer afternoon (85-90° F) - 70 knots indicated is about 87 knots true, and under such conditions if you lift off at your normal 48 to 50 knots indicated, your true airspeed is about 62 knots, which is visually quite apparent as your takeoff roll progresses. So, do not allow that obvious speed to influence your liftoff; reference only your airspeed indicator, an indication reinforced by your *aerodynamic* feel of the machine. Your takeoff roll will be a long one, and you'll be rolling at a high ground speed. Be prepared for that, and lift off at your normal IAS unless, of course, there are obstacles or other considerations to modify your technique.

Because temperature is a controlling factor in the determination of density altitude, high-altitude takeoffs during warm weather are often planned for the relatively cooler morning hours (Figs. 5-8 through 5-10). Such planning beats the winds that are generated by convection activity, and also avoids the thunderstorms that are an almost daily occurrence in the mountains from midday onward in the summertime.

Taking off from an airport with a density altitude of 5,000 feet or greater, flying a normally aspirated engine (not turbocharged), you should

Fig. 5-8. The denalt pocket computer provides takeoff distance and rate of climb at various altitudes and temperatures. Directions for use are printed on the face. There are separate versions for fixed-pitch and variable-pitch propeller installations.

lean the fuel mixture or else suffer a loss in performance from an engine that is already operating at least 15° below its rated power. There is a small problem with this. You will be guessing, because you'll be leaning the fuel mixture at magneto-check RPM of 1,700, meaning that you have adjusted the mixture for that engine speed. Pull out the mixture knob until the engine begins to run rough, then push in the mixture to smooth out the engine, perhaps giving it an extra quarter-inch to keep the cylinder heads cool. After takeoff, with your climb established, you may readjust the mixture for the higher power setting.

This procedure is not very precise. The best way to do it is by reference to an exhaust gas temperature (EGT) gauge, along with oil and cylinder-head temperature gauges. Leaning your fuel mixture with an EGT provides a reference point, or peak temperature of the exhaust (the temperature of most complete combustion). Pull out the mixture control until EGT peaks, then enrich to about 150° on the rich side of peak—the extra fuel serving as a coolant (which is why air-cooled engines are not as fuel efficient as liquid-cooled engines). Monitor your cylinder-head and oil temperatures. If they climb out of the green arcs, enrich some more.

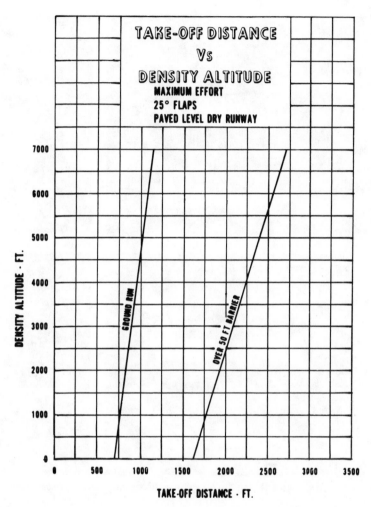

Fig. 5-9. Typical takeoff chart for various density altitudes as given in an airplane owner's manual. *(FAA)*

As a practical matter, your climbout after takeoff from a high-altitude airport will often be whatever conditions (density altitude, winds, surrounding terrain) allow. If there are obstacles to surmount—tall trees, sharply rising terrain, etc.—a check of your owner's manual prior to takeoff should reveal that your best-angle-of-climb speed increases with altitude, while your best-rate-of-climb speed drops. The manufacturer's engineering test pilots went to a lot of trouble to draw the graphs and compile the tables in the owner's manual; use those data. And add 10%, because it's unlikely that you will get the same performance from the airplane that they did.

A common problem at high-altitude airports is engine overheating due to prolonged operation on the ground before takeoff. At idle and taxi

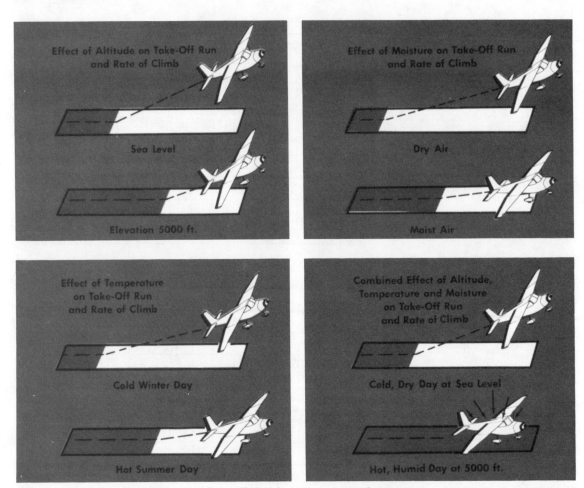

Fig. 5-10. Conditions affecting the takeoff run. *(Copyright 1986 Jeppesen Sanderson, Inc. Reprinted with permission.)*

speeds you don't have the volume of air flowing around the cylinder that they receive down in the flatlands.

Wet and Icy

A takeoff may be questionable when one-third or more of the runway is covered by as little as ½ inch of water, wet snow, or slush. I don't mean one-third of the runway all at one end—you probably can avoid that. What I'm talking about here is patches of such stuff. Each time you hit a patch of slush it's analogous to a sudden application of brakes. Approaching takeoff velocity and ploughing into a large puddle of water or patch of slush may slam the nosewheel into the mush with enough force to damage that vulnerable component and/or start a severe swerve—the latter especially when one main hits the slush and one does not.

Lesser depths of water or wet snow may be overcome, although you must add up to 20% to your normal takeoff run. Common sense is really your final guide, and it's probably worth the effort to select an accelerate/stop point along the runway where, if you have not attained liftoff velocity it's time to shut down and abort the takeoff. Selecting the accelerate/stop point is not hard if you have equally spaced runway lights to use in determining distance, or a taxiway of known distance from the threshold, etc. Consult your owner's manual for the takeoff distance required in the prevailing density altitude conditions and add 20% to that for surface conditions. Then ask yourself if there is room enough to stop beyond your accelerate/stop point.

In cold weather, water or slush on the runway, even in small amounts, can be splashed into the wheel wells of retractables and packed into the wheel pants (speed fairings) of fixed-gear airplanes—there to freeze in the colder air aloft after takeoff. I don't need to tell you about the interesting events to follow when it comes time to lower the gear and land. Leave the gear down following takeoff until the wheel wells are dried. The only way to ensure that wheels do not freeze inside tight-fitting wheel pants is to remove them for the winter (the pants, not the wheels!).

A refreeze danger is also present when an ice-covered airplane that has been tied down out-of-doors is rolled into a heated hangar to prepare

Fig. 5-11. A re-freeze danger is present when an ice-covered airplane is rolled into a heated hangar to prepare it for flight. Melted ice and snow can drain into control surface wells, or into the flight controls themselves, and re-freeze in flight. Ethylene glycol is the best ice remover if applied hot; but its effectiveness is questionable if applied cold. The aircraft pictured is a Champion Lancer.

Fig. 5-12. Even a light coating of frost significantly increases an airplane's stalling speed; it's not the weight, but the drag.

it for flight. Ice and snow that have melted and drained into surface wells and hinges can refreeze during or following takeoff and interfere with the operation of the flight controls at a critical time. Pay particular attention to control surface drain/ventilation holes to make sure that trapped water does not remain inside an elevator or aileron to freeze later in flight resulting in imbalance and flutter which could lead to failure (Figs. 5-11 and 5-12). Such a condition brought down a Learjet several years ago.

Soft-field techniques are best in almost all snow and slush conditions. If the snow is too deep to allow the airplane to accelerate, you can sometimes make several runs down the same tracks to pack the snow, but there is nothing you can do with slush or water when there is enough of it to impede your takeoff run.

In areas where the snow lasts all winter, some lightplane pilots switch to skis during the cold months rather than place their machines in storage until spring. That kind of flying is different enough to require a checkout by an experienced skiplane instructor. There are other considerations, not the least of which is where your airplane is parked. If you have ever tried to open T-hangar doors with bottom rollers encased in a couple of inches of ice, or if you have asked yourself what you were doing on a snow-covered deserted airport contemplating an engine pre-heater rendered useless by a dead electrical outlet, you may have decided that winter storage for your personal airplane isn't such a dumb idea after all.

6

Emergency Landings

MANY OF TODAY'S CIVILIAN PILOTS ARE SO CONDITIONED TO PAVED RUN-ways that reach halfway to their destination that they give little thought to the possibility of an off-airport emergency landing. But someone makes an emergency or precautionary landing every day. Despite the oft-repeated myth that today's lightplane engines are so highly developed that engine failure is almost unheard of, the fact is that these engines do fail. It has happened to me, and it recently happened to my colleague Don Downie and his wife Julia (in a brand new airplane!).

Engines fail because something breaks internally—valve heads break off, crankshafts part, accessory gears are chewed up—and some of the failures are due to poor or improper maintenance, some to defective parts (the modern automobile engine is better built). An amazing number of lightplane engine failures are due to the fact that all the gasoline in the airplane's fuel tanks has been replaced by air (Fig. 6-1).

But engine problems are not the only reasons for off-airport landings. Nor are all off-airport landings "forced" landings. Some are precautionary, made in the face of deteriorating weather, or while a small problem, threatening to become worse, is still manageable.

The FAA says that some people are killed or injured in lightplanes because of their reluctance to accept the unpleasant possibilities inherent in airborne emergencies. They say that a desire to save the airplane and an "undue" concern about getting hurt are the factors which lead to

91

Fig. 6-1. You always visually check the fuel tanks because you want to smell the fuel (to make sure it is not jet fuel), see its color (to verify proper grade), and confirm quantity (because you cannot completely trust the gauges or the gas jockeys). *(FAA)*

indecision and poor decisions when a situation pumps the cockpit ankle deep in adrenaline. In other words, be prepared to meet your responsibilities as pilot-in-command, and act.

It is possible to plan most of your emergency landing procedure in advance. Make an emergency checklist, keep it handy, and when the time comes, follow it, item by item. Also in advance, learn how various possible landing sites appear from the air at different times of the year. A plowed field is a plowed field, but the color of the soil can differ in different parts of the country, and in the West and Southwest it is often soft with irrigation water. A superficial knowledge of regional agricultural conditions may therefore help in your selection of an emergency landing field and also aid you in deciding whether to land wheels-ups or wheels-down. Cultivated fields are usually satisfactory, and plowed fields are acceptable if the landing is made parallel to the furrows. If irrigated, however, a high-wing machine with gear down will probably end up on its back, so it would not be my first choice in a Cessna single.

Without power, it's probably best to look for the biggest field you can find, then consider wind direction (Fig. 6-2). The amount of altitude you have when the fan stops is going to determine how much time you have for the several things that must be done, and several important things will have to wait. You can't select your field from 10,000 feet, and you aren't going to deploy flaps until absolutely certain that you have your field made.

Fig. 6-2. Engines do quit. The pilot of this restored Spartan C-3 is gliding for a likely looking pasture below. His landing was uneventful.

Ground obstructions can make landing into the wind undesirable because they subtract from the available field length; you may not have enough altitude to maneuver for a landing into the wind, and a landing downhill into the wind may be worse than a crosswind or downwind landing. Take the wind if you can get it, but terrain and obstacle considerations come first, as does the simple need to *reach* your selected landing field.

If you have enough altitude, fly a standard traffic pattern, although without power you may want to make a smaller, tighter, and higher pattern than usual. The pattern allows you a good look at your selected field, and it aids in judging distances because it's a familiar procedure. Besides, you'll probably be approaching from downwind anyway, because the selection of a field that is downwind when the emergency develops ensures the maximum distance you can cover before reaching the ground, thereby multiplying your options.

Failed-Engine Procedure

Mentioned earlier was the suggestion that you have a plan for inflight power failure and a prepared checklist to follow. Your first action will always be to establish your most efficient glide speed. From that instant until the airplane comes to a stop on the ground your primary concern is to *fly the airplane*. Depending upon altitude, you then either go through your engine-failure checklist or pick your landing field. Your checklist will start with the application of carburetor heat (with a dead engine, there won't be carb heat for long, and probably not enough to melt carburetor throat ice in any case, but it doesn't do any harm). Check the fuel selector switch, and cycle it to make sure that it rests in the indent it is pointed to and that it is turned to the fullest tank. Turn on the fuel pump, mixture to full rich, and cycle the ignition switch, returning it to BOTH. If the propeller is windmilling, try a shot of primer, and if you have no restart by this time, move the propeller control to low RPM (if appropriate) to minimize drag. Finally, turn your communications radio to 121.5 and squawk 7700 on your transponder.

Your best glide airspeed, that is, the airspeed which will take you the most distance, should be listed on your engine-failure checklist, and you will find it in your owner's manual. If you don't have it, use V_y, your best-rate-of-climb airspeed; it'll be close. V_x will keep you up longer, with the slowest rate-of-descent, but I can think of no use for it until on a short final, under some conditions.

With your descent speed stabilized, re-trim, and then make your call on 121.5: "Mayday, mayday, mayday." Identify yourself in your usual way. Then give your position, the nature of your problem, and your intentions. That's all they need. Repeat your call if you have time, and if you have plenty of altitude you may ask for a vector and the distance to the nearest airport. Otherwise, *concentrate on flying your airplane* and keep distractions—including unnecessary conversation with ATC—to a minimum.

It is advisable to keep your speed up until you are sure that you will reach your selected landing patch. High and fast on final is adjustable, but without power there's nothing you can do if you're low and slow. Usually, you will be using short-field technique from that point.

Whatever technique the situation dictates, always consider that your airplane is expendable in the interest of occupant protection. The FAA says that, as long as the cabin remains intact, and you strike no immovable object head-on at a significant speed, serious injury is unlikely in a crash (Fig. 6-3). Those long wings out there are energy absorbers. Don't hesitate to use them as such.

Engine Failure on Takeoff

If your engine should fail shortly after liftoff and before you have attained a safe maneuvering altitude—500 feet absolute minimum at V_y in most lightplanes, pattern altitude or 800 feet at V_x—it is inadvisable to attempt to turn back to the field from which you took off. It is usually safer to immediately turn off all electrical, ignition, and fuel switches, establish a glide straight ahead, select a place to land that is no more than 15° to either side of your track, and *concentrate on flying the airplane*. Positive control is your key to an injury-free crash landing.

The decision to continue straight ahead is often a difficult one, but again, preplanning can help. At your home field, and at others that you regularly visit, study the areas off the ends of the runways and ask yourself where you could land down there if you had to. During the early fall of 1985, I had arranged an interview with Chris Beachner, who was flying a Buick V-8 engine in his homebuilt off the Eloy (Arizona) Municipal Airport. I arrived to discover that Chris had been killed two days before when he attempted a 180-degree turn following engine failure on takeoff. I also recall that, shortly before Word War II, my original instructor, along with Tom Braniff's son, were killed when they tried the same thing at Oklahoma City.

The so-called 180-following-engine-failure-soon-after-takeoff has claimed a lot of lives before and since then. In the first place, it is not really a 180. A 180-degree turn would put you parallel to the runway, but not *on* it. To return to the runway, two turns would be required—a 270 and an opposing 90. That's a bit much without power at low altitude. As the record shows, the "180" under these conditions is a trap.

Fig. 6-3. The first rule of the emergency landing is to *maintain control* of the airplane. As long as the cabin remains intact, the rest of the machine is expendable. Stall, and you end up like this.

Also keep in mind that, to return to the takeoff field, a downwind turn must be made. That suddenly increases your ground speed, which in turn can easily cause you to hurry the turn, and you know the fatal sequence this can lead to—a hurried turn, crossed controls, low speed, low altitude . . .

Fire

The rarest of all forced landings is one due to fire. It is also the scariest. A lady I know opened the cabin door of her little Cessna 140 and jumped out onto the runway as smoke came billowing from beneath the engine cowling during the takeoff run. She had just begun to roll and therefore was only bruised and shaken. She also had the presence of mind to cut the switch, which saved the airplane. The smoke was generated by a bird's nest erected between two cylinders and a portion of the exhaust manifold.

Inflight fires are practically unheard of because proper maintenance eliminates the causes—leaking fuel lines, cracked manifolds, and accumulations of dirt and oil in the engine compartment. There is nothing in the engine compartment to burn except the fuel being routed through the carburetor and intakes. As long as the plumbing connectors and lines are secure, and the engine cowling inner surface and firewall are kept clean, the possibility of fire is remote indeed.

If you should experience that one-in-a-million inflight fire, your options are obviously limited. Just do as the old-timers did in their more flammable machines: Turn the fuel selector to OFF, the master and magneto switches to OFF, and side-slip the airplane to blow the fire away from the cabin. With the fuel supply cut off, there's a good chance that you will blow out the fire and/or starve it. Continue the slip to get on the ground as soon as possible. The side-slip is performed the same as a forward slip, except that you hold the nose a little higher and use rudder to achieve the angle you want.

You understand, I'm working from second-hand intelligence on this subject. I don't even *know* anyone who has ever had an engine fire in flight (except from battle damage in World War II, and the drill then was simply to bail out). But clearly, the way to beat engine fires in flight in lightplanes is through good maintenance and a thorough inspection of your machine prior to the first flight of the day.

Smoke in the cabin during flight is almost always due to an electrical problem, and the common sense remedy is to cut off all electrics (except the ignition, of course) and land at the nearest airport. Open your storm window and ventilate the cabin. Don't worry about ''fanning'' the fire; you cannot risk smoke inhalation and the certain loss of control that would bring.

If you carry a fire extinguisher in your airplane, make sure that you know what it contains. Carry only one that uses Halon as an extinguishing agent as per the FAA Advisory Circular AC 20-42C. This is the least toxic type and is effective against gasoline as well as electrical fires. It leaves no residue and will not damage expensive avionics.

By now, it will be hard to find a fabric-covered airplane finished in the old highly-flammable cellulose nitrate dope, so that danger is a thing of the past. Cellulose acetate butyrate dope will burn, but won't sustain a live flame in flight.

The Precautionary Landing

A lot of people who are now statistics would be alive today had they not been so reluctant to face up to a bad situation and possessed the good sense to make a precautionary landing. I've heard it called a "chicken landing" by some of the hot rocks; but for my part, when I see the choice as being between "stupid" and "chicken," I'd rather be classed as chicken. I've known some scud-runners and others—including some otherwise very intelligent people—who could never be called "chicken"— but they can be called very dead.

There are many situations in addition to deteriorating weather that can make it highly desirable to return to earth, posthaste, as they say. These include impending darkness, a dwindling fuel supply, and being "temporarily lost," or a combination of these conditions (airborne problems have a way of piling up); it's usually not the first one or two that get you, it's what they lead to—all of which are normally traceable to careless planning.

A precautionary landing is no big deal if you can find an airport close by, which is not too difficult if you have a clue as to where you are. And an off-airport landing *under positive control*, including a slightly bent airplane, sure beats what too often happens when a non-instrument pilot tries to "push the weather" or flies his fuel to exhaustion before looking for a place to land.

A Final Word

The FAA manuals show us how to make power-off emergency landings, but in those examples the airplane is well-positioned when power is retarded, the weather is good, the winds are light, the wind direction is known, and the field selected is large and level with no rocks, trees, or ditches to complicate things. In real life you aren't likely to get all those breaks. The *only* available field from your relatively low altitude may be upwind and reachable (hopefully) by way of a straight-in approach. Most of us find a long straight-in approach more difficult to judge than when establishing a final from well-practiced downwind and base legs, especially when surface wind direction and velocity are uncertain factors.

Also, once your engine develops a terminal case of the quiets, the standard short-field technique might be too much of a gamble because you are too close to stalling speed for full flaps on final approach. Without power, 20–25° of flaps, along with a minimum airspeed of 1.3 V_{so}, is more practical. Full flaps pitch the nose down too steeply, and the airplane will stop flying too suddenly at the stall. Without power you are much better off to be a few knots too fast because *positive control* is your single most important consideration. To put it another way, it's better to run into obstacles at the far end of the field at 10 knots than to smash into them at the approach end at 50 knots.

7

Communicate

WE CAN ALL THINK OF FOULED-UP SITUATIONS THAT WERE CAUSED BY poor communications. One of my favorite examples happened during World War II. A Navy student pilot reported that he had seen an N3N trainer, buzz number so-and-so, making an emergency landing in a farm field some 20 miles from the Naval Air Station. The downed pilot's instructor, one of those I-can-fly-a-barn-door-if-it's-got-an-engine types, climbed into another N3N and flew to the site of the forced landing to assess the damage and retrieve his student.

Upon arrival, the instructor was dismayed to find the disabled airplane in an incredibly small field that was bounded by a low rock fence. He circled, noting that a much larger field was adjacent to the one containing the downed machine which, by the way, was clearly undamaged. The instructor gave scant consideration to the obviously more appropriate field. If that solo student could squeeze an N3N into such a space . . .

Well, you guessed it; the instructor smashed a wing into the rock fence opposite his touchdown point as he attempted a last-second ground loop to avoid striking the fence head-on.

He climbed from the cockpit and strode purposefully toward his student. "Mister," he said, struggling to control himself, "Tell me exactly how you managed to land in this (expletive deleted) pea patch?"

"I didn't exactly land here, sir." The student gestured toward the adjacent field. "I landed over there and sort of bounced over here."

That instructor could have avoided the damage to his airplane and embarrassment to himself had he bothered to seek additional details of the forced landing from the cadet who reported it, or by radio from the one who performed it. A little communication would have made a lot of difference.

On a more somber note, I'm reminded of the 1977 collision between two Boeing 747s which killed 582 people on a fog-shrouded runway at Tenerife in the Canary Islands. That one happened because both captains believed they had been cleared for takeoff. One had not.

So, the kind of communication I am talking about here implies complete understanding, among the crew members, and between the crew and the controlling authorities on the ground. Specifically, we are concerned with communications attendant to airport and traffic pattern operations in visual meteorological conditions. By extension, that may include flight planning, but I will focus on the use of your aircraft radio: Whom to call, when, how, and why.

Radio Phraseology

The "how" means the use of acceptable phraseology as well as tuning the proper frequency. It's true that controllers would rather hear from a pilot who stumbles through a radio transmission, repeating himself and tying up the frequency for several minutes with a message that could have been given in five to ten seconds, than not hear from him at all. But the pilot who has thus identified himself as an inconsiderate amateur is increasingly, these days, receiving less and less consideration from busy controllers. Although he may meet the legal requirements for entry into a TCA, a busy controller may tell him to remain clear of the TCA, not only to free the radio frequency, but to avoid mixing a pilot of questionable ability with the other traffic. Mostly, it is because the controller lacks the time to bother with the pilot who has failed to learn the proper use of his communications radio.

There are those who take the position that their tax money is paying for the air traffic control system, including controllers' salaries, and therefore the burden is on the controllers to "do their jobs." That isn't exactly the way it is. First of all, your relationship with the controllers is 50-50; you do your share, they do theirs. The system will not work without pilot cooperation (Fig. 7-1). Secondly, while it is true that the controller is there to serve you, he or she is also there to serve all those other taxpayers who have radios in their airplanes. Once again, the key is courtesy and consideration for the other guy. And, once again, that translates into safe flying.

Fig. 7-1. Restored Meyers OTW biplane without radio is permitted to land at a controlled airport for display because the pilot phoned ahead. Controllers knew when to expect the Meyers and cleared it with light-gun signals.

I should mention that pilots often do not use the FAA-recommended phraseology when using their communication radios, but employ something close which has gained acceptance because it is brief and because controllers understand it. An example is reference to altitudes. While the controller will say, for example, "five thousand five hundred" or "eight thousand five hundred," many pilots will say, "five point five" or "eight point five"—which the controllers seem to accept without complaint. But someday, there is bound to be a fatal misunderstanding as a result of such inventiveness; not because it is not sufficiently descriptive, but because pilot and controller are assigning different terms to a common concept.

The term "over" isn't heard much anymore. It means that your message is complete and that you expect a reply. The nature of your message is usually enough to establish whether or not a reply is expected. If you think there could be any doubt, add "over" at the end.

Never acknowledge a controller's directive with a simple "Roger." The controller may be in contact with several aircraft, and he or she has no way of knowing whose "Roger" it is. Acknowledge with the aircraft type (e.g. Cessna, Cherokee, etc.) and the last three digits of your N-number (assuming that your initial contact included your complete N-number, and that the controller has responded to you using the abbreviated call sign. Otherwise, use your complete N-number, because the controller apparently is in contact with an aircraft using an N-number that could be confused with yours).

Never hesitate to ask a controller to "say again" if you do not completely understand a directive. As always, a little common sense goes a long way. If, for example, Ground Control has directed you to a runway for takeoff that is reached by crossing another runway, make sure that you understand that message. If there is any doubt at all, repeat the taxi instructions back to the controller. Never allow your desire for brevity to compromise total understanding between you and a controller. You don't have to get smashed crossing that intervening runway in order to regret that you did not clarify your instructions. Taxiing across a runway without a controller's permission can get you into serious trouble with the FAA.

While on the subject of trouble with the FAA, a timely tip is in order: As a result of recent pressure by the news media on the FAA over the questions of air safety in general, and alleged pilot laxity in particular, air traffic controllers have begun reporting even those lesser pilot transgressions that used to be handled by a request from the tower to "come up for a talk." Fines and temporary suspension of pilot certificates seem to be replacing the friendly warnings.

To continue our discussion on aircraft radiotelephone phraseology, begin each transmission with the name of the facility being called:

Approach Control — "Albuquerque Approach"

Ground Control — "Wichita Ground"

Control Tower — "Lawton Tower"

Flight Service Station — "Hanford Radio"

UNICOM — "Hobart UNICOM"

The name of the facility being called is immediately followed by your identification, which is the aircraft type and its N-number, followed by your request:

"Wichita Ground, Cessna Five Niner Two Seven Juliet, at Yingling Aircraft, taxi to Learjet."

You told him where you are and that you want to taxi around the terminal to the north edge of the airport where Learjet is located. Had you been ready to depart the airport and needed taxi instructions to the proper runway, you would have said:

"Wichita Ground, Cessna Five Niner Two Seven Juliet, at Yingling Aircraft, ready to taxi, VFR to Dallas, with Information Foxtrot."

"Foxtrot," for "F" in the phonetic air radiotelephone alphabet, is the coded age of the Automatic Terminal Information Service (ATIS) broadcast. ATIS is a recording by tower personnel, transmitted continuously, which provides basic airport and meteorological data at major airports. It is normally updated each hour, and each succeeding ATIS advances one letter. When you tell the controller which ATIS you have monitored—Foxtrot, in the above example—the controller knows whether or not you have the latest one.

Typically, an ATIS broadcast provides the time (UTC or "Zulu"), ceiling and visibility (if better than 5,000 feet and five miles, it may be omitted), obstructions to visibility, temperature and dew point; wind, altimeter setting, runways in use, current NOTAMs, plus AIRMETs and SIGMETs in adverse weather. The purpose of these recordings is to free the controllers from the need to repeat this data for each arriving and departing aircraft, giving them more time to ensure the safe separation of the air traffic.

The ATIS radio frequencies are shown on Sectional charts just below the control tower frequencies.

Ground Control frequencies are not shown on Sectionals. Obtain them from the Flight Service Station specialist when you get your weather briefing, from the FBO when you pay your bill, or preferably, from the *Airport/Facility Directory (A/FD)*. Normally, Ground Control will be in the 121.6 through 121.9 band. After landing, tower will usually supply the Ground Control frequency. Do not leave the tower frequency until told to do so.

Uncontrolled Airports

Takeoff from an airport which has no tower does not relieve you of the need to communicate. Always use the Common Traffic Advisory

Frequency (CTAF) listed in the *A/FD*. If there is a Flight Service Station on the field, the CTAF will probably be 123.6. If there is no Flight Service Station, the CTAF will usually be the UNICOM frequency (it's on the Sectional charts and will be in the band width of 122.7 through 123.0 inclusive). If there is no tower, no Flight Service Station, and no UNICOM, transmit your intentions on MULTICOM (122.9). If the tower is closed, the CTAF will usually be the tower frequency. The important thing is to let other air traffic in the area know what you are doing—that is, where you are and where you intend to be in that shared airspace.

How can you be sure that whatever traffic is out there is guarding the proper frequency? You cannot, but that does not relieve your obligation to operate safely. Besides, the pilot who *is* monitoring your call may be the one who didn't see you in the pattern.

Approach Communications. When approaching a field which has no tower, tune to the appropriate CTAF about 10–15 miles out. You may hear others operating from the field and learn the wind and active runway. Then you can announce your own position and intentions. If there is a UNICOM or Flight Service Station on the field you can obtain local airport advisories—runway, wind, altimeter, and known traffic. If the UNICOM does not reply, transmit in the blind (the FAA calls it "self-announce," which makes no sense), and address the transmission to "Traffic." For example, "Hobart Traffic, Cessna Five Niner Two Seven Juliet, ten miles southeast at two thousand five hundred. Will enter pattern upwind for Runway Three Six, Hobart."

As you enter the pattern (anyone already in the pattern has the right-of-way), identify yourself and give your position and intentions once again. Do this whether or not there is any other traffic. The fact that you don't see any is all the more reason to keep the world informed of your presence and intentions.

Report your turn from downwind to base leg, from base to final, and, once on the ground, again transmit your identity and position. If the airport is small and you have to back-taxi on the active, broadcast the news that you are doing so.

Controlled Airports

Every airport that has an operating control tower automatically has an Airport Traffic Area (ATA) surrounding it which always has a radius of five statute miles from the center of the airport, and which extends upward to, but not including, 3,000 feet AGL. When the tower is not in operation, the ATA does not exist. ATAs are not shown on charts. You must be in radio contact with the tower in order to enter an ATA, and you should make your initial call at least 10 miles from the ATA.

Control Zones

Control Zones (CZs) are shown on your Sectional chart. They vary in shape (many have the shape of a keyhole) because they include extensions for IFR arrivals and departures. CZs extend upward to 14,500 feet, the base of the Continental Control Area, and many surround airports that have no control towers, but a Flight Service Station or weather reporting station. You must obtain a Special VFR clearance to enter a Control Zone when the ceiling is less than 1,000 feet and/or the visibility is less than 3 miles.

There has been some confusion about CZs at airports without control towers (and therefore no ATA). The key is the VFR minimums. You may enter (or depart from) a CZ where the weather is 1,000-and-3 or better without contacting the controlling authority.

TRSAs, ARSAs, TCAs

The air traffic control system in the U.S. is a patchwork of add-on rules and procedures. Year by year, controlled airspace is added-on, new regulations are added-on, and new technology is added-on. There has never been an overall, integrated plan. That's bound to spawn some confusion.

The *Terminal Radar Service Area* (TRSA) imposes no restrictions for VFR aircraft. It is simply an optional radar service for VFR pilots provided only on a "controller workload permitting" basis. So, the TRSA as presently offered is more confusin' than amusin'. On aeronautical charts, it is indicated by a set of solid magenta concentric "quasi-circles" (Fig. 7-2). TRSAs are being replaced by ARSAs in many locations.

The *Airport Radar Service Area* (ARSA), shown on aeronautical charts by slashed magenta circles (Fig. 7-3) is perhaps best understood by referencing the FAA drawing (Fig. 7-4), and consists of two circular blocks of airspace normally 4,000 feet in height, centered over the airport. The inner circle has a radius of 5 NM and begins at the surface. The outer circle has a radius of 10 NM and begins at 1,200 feet above the surface. An "outer area" possessing a radius of 20 NM surrounds the two smaller blocks of airspace. Pilot participation is mandatory within the ARSA, but optional in the so-called outer area.

The *Terminal Control Area* (TCA) is always described as resembling an upside-down wedding cake, sometimes with a slice or two taken from it. Each circular layer of airspace, although larger in diameter than the one below it, may not be perfectly round. You must reference your Sectional chart for a general view of each TCA, and then study the special Terminal Area Charts in order to determine the dimensions of each layer.

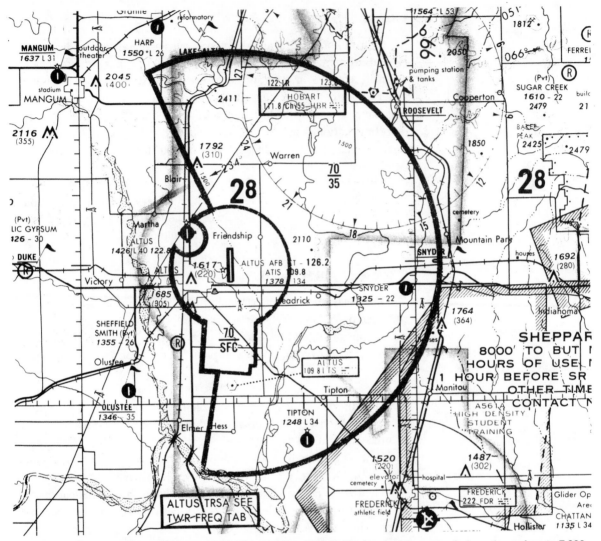

Fig. 7-2. The Altus (Oklahoma) Terminal Radar Service Area (TRSA). The inner portion extends from the surface to 7,000 feet; the outer portion from 3,500 to 7,000 feet. Altus Municipal is outside of both.

TCAs are not standardized. The top layer of TCA airspace is, of course, the largest and caps all the rest.

On your Sectionals, TCAs are indicated by solid blue lines (Fig. 7-5). Until recently, there were 23 TCAs, but nine more have been proposed.

Currently, the requirements for entering a TCA are a 4096-code transponder with Mode C, a VOR receiver, and an operating two-way radio with all the necessary ATC frequencies. To land or depart from the primary TCA airport the pilot must hold at least a private pilot certificate. (At this writing this last requirement applies only at the busier "Group I" TCAs, but may soon be extended to cover all TCAs.)

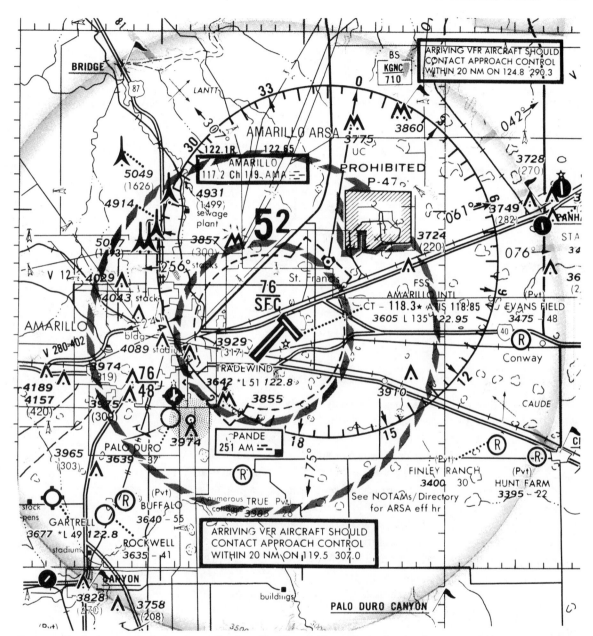

Fig. 7-3. Slashed magenta circles denote the Amarillo (Texas) Airport Radar Service Area. It extends from the surface to 7,600 feet within the inner circle and from 4,800 to 7,600 feet in the outer circle.

These are the *minimum* requirements. Then, *if* you sound as if you know what you are doing when you contact the tower, the controller may clear you to enter the TCA. After that, you must be able to fly your airplane with a reasonable degree of precision and employ the proper aviation radio phraseology.

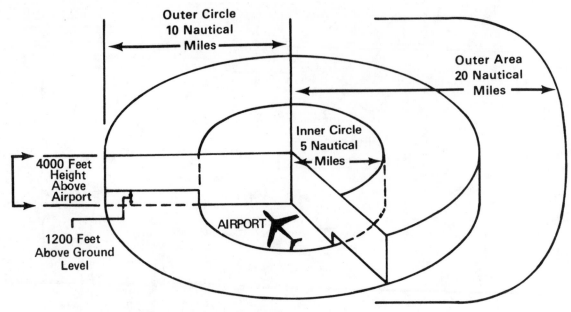

Fig. 7-4. Three dimensional schematic of a typical ARSA.

Radio Procedures for Entering the TCA

When your destination is the major terminal underlying a TCA, make your initial radio call to Approach Control while still outside the TCA. Do not penetrate any layer of the TCA until you are cleared to do so. The top layer of the TCA may be 20 miles or so from the airport. Note that the top layer of the Dallas TCA (Fig. 7-5) is 40 NM across, has an upper limit of 8,000 feet and a floor of 5,000 feet—except for a hunk on the north edge which has a floor of 4,000 ft. Little bits of the first layer atop the core have a floor of 2,000 feet, while the odd-shaped layer above it appears to have a floor of 3,000 feet (the $^{80}\!/_{30}$ just above the Love Field box), and the southeast quadrant has another piece of airspace with a 4,000 foot floor. Perhaps you can tell from this example why pilots who fly only occasionally to major terminals have trouble figuring out just where in the hell the TCA floors and outer limits happen to be. Clearly, the safest procedure is to make your initial call while still outside the lateral limits of the top layer.

Approach Control will vector you into the TCA until the tower controller takes over to give pattern and landing directives. Tower in turn will hand you off to Ground Control once you are down and on the taxiway. Do not change radio frequencies until told to do so. Because most ground control frequencies are in the 121.6 through 121.9

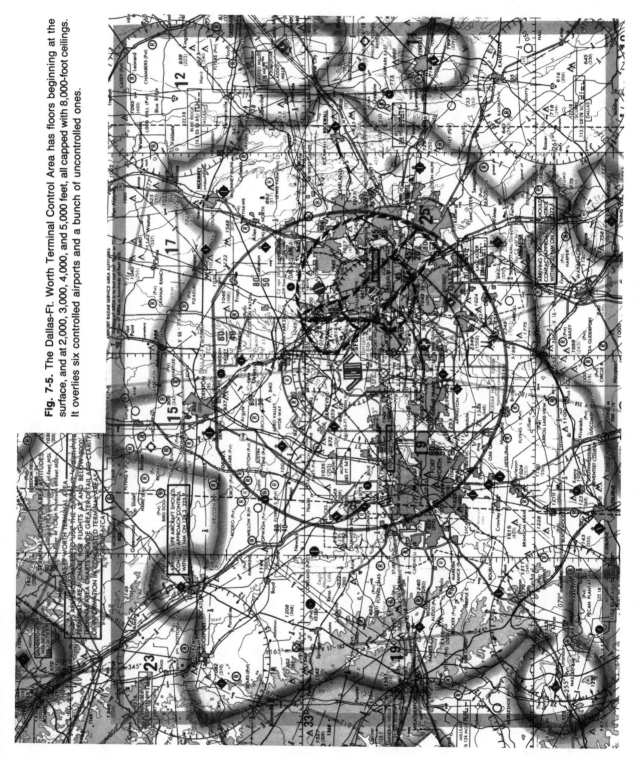

Fig. 7-5. The Dallas-Ft. Worth Terminal Control Area has floors beginning at the surface, and at 2,000, 3,000, 4,000, and 5,000 feet, all capped with 8,000-foot ceilings. It overlies six controlled airports and a bunch of uncontrolled ones.

bandwidth, many controllers will omit the numbers preceding the decimal point. For example, for 121.7 the controller may say, "Contact Ground point seven." Tower and Approach Control frequencies are on Sectionals and Terminal Area Charts.

Appendices

Appendix A

Selected Abbreviations, FAR Part 1

"ADF" means automatic direction finder.

"AGL" means above ground level.

"ALS" means approach light system.

"ASR" means airport surveillance radar.

"ATC" means air traffic control.

"CAS" means calibrated airspeed.

"CAT II" means Category II.

"DH" means decision height.

"DME" means distance measuring equipment compatible with TACAN.

"FAA" means Federal Aviation Administration.

"GS" means glideslope.

"HIRL" means high-intensity runway light system.

"IAS" means indicated airspeed.

"IFR" means instrument flight rules.

"ILS" means instrument landing system.

"IM" means ILS inner marker.

"INT" means intersection.

"LDA" means localizer-type directional aid.

"LMM" means compass locator at the middle marker.

"LOC" means ILS localizer.

"LOM" means compass locator at the outer marker.

"MAA" means maximum authorized IFR altitude.

"MALS" means medium intensity approach light system.

"MALSR" means medium intensity approach light system with runway alignment indicator lights.

"MCA" means minimum crossing altitude.

"MDA" means minimum descent altitude.

"MEA" means minimum en route IFR altitude.

"MM" means ILS middle marker.

"MOCA" means minimum obstruction clearance altitude.

"MRA" means minimum reception altitude.

"MSL" means mean sea level.

"NDB" means nondirectional beacon.

"NOPT" means no procedure turn required.

"OM" means outer marker.

"PAR" means precision approach radar.

"RAIL" means runway alignment indicator light system.

"RCLM" means runway centerline marking.

"RCLS" means runway centerline light system.

"REIL" means runway end identification lights.

"RVR" means runway visual range as measured in the touch-down area.

"SALS" means short approach light system.

"SSALS" means simplified short approach light system.

"SSALSR" means simplified short approach light system with runway alignment indicator lights plus coffee and doughnuts.

"TACAN" means ultra-high frequency tactical air navigation aid.

"TAS" means true airspeed.

"TDZL" means touchdown zone lights.

"TVOR" means very high frequency terminal omnirange station.

"V_a" means design maneuvering speed.

"V_b" means design speed for maximum gust intensity.

"V_c" means design cruising speed.

"V_d" means design diving speed.

"V_{df}/M_{df}" means demonstrated flight diving speed.

"V_f" means design flap speed.

"V_{fc}/M_{fc}" means maximum speed for stability characteristics.

"V_{fe}" means maximum flap extended speed.

"V_h" means maximum speed in level flight with maximum continuous power.

"V_{le}" means maximum landing gear extended speed.

"V_{lo}" means maximum landing gear operating speed.

"V_{lof}" means liftoff speed.

"V_{mc}" means minimum control speed with the critical engine inoperative.

"V_{mo}/M_{mo}" means maximum operating limit speed.

"V_{mu}" means minimum unstick speed.

"V_{ne}" means never exceed speed.

"V_{no}" means maximum structural cruising speed.

"V_r" means rotation speed.

"V_s" means the stalling speed or the minimum steady flight speed at which the airplane is controllable.

"V_{so}" means the stalling speed or the minimum steady flight speed in the landing configuration.

"V_{s1}" means the stalling speed or the minimum steady flight speed obtained in a specific configuration.

"V_x" means speed for best angle of climb.

"V_y" means speed for the best rate of climb.

"V_1" means takeoff decision speed (formerly denoted as critical engine failure speed).

"V_2" means takeoff safety speed.

"$V_{2\,min}$" means minimum takeoff safety speed.

"VFR" means visual flight rules.

"VHF" means very high frequency.

"VOR" means very high frequency omnirange station.

"VORTAC" means co-located VOR and TACAN.

Appendix B

Selected Definitions, FAR Part 1

Airport traffic area means, unless otherwise specifically designated in Part 93, that airspace within a horizontal radius of five statute miles from the geographical center of any airport at which a control tower is operating, extending from the surface up to, but not including, 3,000 feet above the elevation of the airport.

Air traffic clearance means an authorization by air traffic control, for the purpose of preventing collision between known aircraft, for an aircraft to proceed under specified traffic conditions within controlled airspace.

Alternate airport means an airport at which an aircraft may land if a landing at the intended airport becomes inadvisable.

Calibrated airspeed means the indicated airspeed of an aircraft, corrected for position and instrument error. Calibrated airspeed is equal to true airspeed in standard atmosphere at sea level.

Category

(1) As used with respect to the certification, ratings, privileges, and limitations of airmen, means a broad classification of aircraft. Examples include: airplane, rotorcraft, glider, and lighter-than-air; and

(2) As used with the respect to the certification of aircraft, means a grouping of aircraft based upon intended use or operating limitations. Examples include: transport, normal, utility, aerobatic, limited, restricted, and provisional.

Category II operations with respect to the operation of aircraft, means a straight-in ILS approach to the runway of an airport under a Category II ILS instrument approach procedure issued by the Administrator or other appropriate authority.

Category III operations with respect to the operation of aircraft, means an ILS approach to, and landing on, the runway of an airport using a Category III ILS instrument approach procedure issued by the Administrator or other appropriate authority.

Ceiling means the height above the earth's surface of the lowest layer of clouds or obscuring phenomena that is reported as "broken," or "overcast," or "obscuration," and not classified as "thin" or "partial."

Class

(1) As used with respect to the certification, ratings, privileges, and limitations of airmen, means a classification of aircraft within a category having similar operating characteristics. Examples include: single-engine; multi-engine; land; water; gyroplane; helicopter; airship; and free balloon; and

(2) As used with respect to the certification of aircraft, means a broad grouping of aircraft having similar characteristics of propulsion, flight, or landing. Examples include: airplane; rotorcraft; glider; balloon; landplane; and seaplane.

Controlled airspace means airspace designated as a continental control area, control area, control zone, terminal control area, or transition area, within which some or all aircraft may be subject to air traffic control.

Decision height, with respect to the operation of aircraft, means the height at which a decision must be made, during an ILS or PAR instrument approach, to either continue the approach or to execute a missed approach.

Flap extended speed means the highest speed permissible with wing flaps in a prescribed extended position.

Flight level means a level of constant atmospheric pressure related to a reference datum of 29.92 inches of mercury (Hg). Each is stated in three digits that represent hundreds of feet. For example, flight level 250 represents a barometric altimeter indication of 25,000 feet; flight level 255, an indication of 25,500 feet.

Flight visibility means the average forward horizontal distance, from the cockpit of an aircraft in flight, at which prominent, unlighted objects may be seen and identified by day and prominent lighted objects may be seen and identified by night.

Ground visibility means prevailing horizontal visibility near the earth's surface as reported by the United States National Weather Service or an accredited observer.

IFR conditions means weather conditions below the minimum for flight under visual flight rules. ["IMC" for instrument meteorological conditions, apparently borrowed from the British, is currently fashionable. It means the same as IFR conditions.]

Indicated airspeed means the speed of an aircraft as shown on its pitot static airspeed indicator calibrated to reflect standard atmosphere adiabatic compressible flow at sea level, uncorrected for airspeed system errors.

Landing gear extended speed means the maximum speed at which an aircraft can be safely flown with the landing gear extended.

Landing gear operating speed means the maximum speed at which the landing gear can be safely extended or retracted.

Large aircraft means aircraft of more than 12,500 pounds maximum certificated takeoff weight.

Lighter-than-air aircraft means aircraft that can rise and remain suspended by using contained gas weighing less than the air that is displaced by the gas.

Load factor means the ratio of a specified load to the total weight of the aircraft. The specified load is expressed in terms of any of the following: aerodynamic forces, inertia forces, or ground or water reactions.

Mach number means the ratio of true airspeed to the speed of sound.

Manifold Pressure means absolute pressure as measured at the appropriate point in the induction system, and usually expressed in inches of mercury.

Minimum descent altitude means the lowest altitude, expressed in feet above mean sea level, to which descent is authorized on final approach or during circle-to-land maneuvering in execution of a standard instrument approach procedure, where no electronic glide slope is provided.

Navigable airspace means airspace at and above the minimum flight altitudes prescribed by or under this chapter [Part 1], including airspace needed for safe takeoff and landing.

Night means the time between the end of evening civil twilight and the beginning of morning civil twilight, as published in the American Air Almanac, converted to local time. [If you are a fan of "Frank and Ernest" in the Sunday comics, then you know that "midnight is when the darkness is directly overhead".]

Nonprecision approach procedure means a standard instrument approach procedure in which no electronic glide slope is provided.

Over-the-top means above the layer of clouds or other obscuring phenomena forming the ceiling.

Pilotage means navigation by visual reference to landmarks.

Pilot in Command means the pilot responsible for the operation and safety of an aircraft during flight time.

Precision approach procedure means a standard instrument approach procedure in which an electronic glide slope is provided, such as ILS and PAR.

Rated maximum continuous power with respect to reciprocating, turbopropeller, and turboshaft engines, means the approved brake horsepower that is developed statically or in flight, in standard atmosphere at a specified altitude, within the engine operating limitations established under Part 33, and approved for unrestricted periods of use.

Rated takeoff power, with respect to reciprocating, turbopropeller, and turboshaft engine type certification, means the approved brake horsepower that is developed statically under standard sea level conditions established under Part 33, and limited in use to periods of not over five minutes for takeoff operation.

Rating means a statement that, as a part of a certificate, sets forth special conditions, privileges, or limitations.

Reporting point means a geographical location in relation to which the position of an aircraft is reported.

Restricted area means airspace designated under Part 73 within which the flight of aircraft, while not wholly prohibited, is subject to restriction.

RNAV way point (W/P) means a predetermined geographical position used for route or instrument approach definition or progress reporting purposes that is defined relative to a VORTAC station position.

Sea level engine means a reciprocating aircraft engine having a rated takeoff power that is attainable only at sea level.

Small aircraft means aircraft of 12,500 pounds or less, maximum certified takeoff weight.

Standard atmosphere means the atmosphere defined in U.S. Standard Atmosphere, 1962 (Geopotential altitude tables).

Stopway means an area beyond the takeoff runway, no less wide than the runway, and centered upon the extended centerline of the runway, able to support the airplane during an aborted takeoff, without causing structural damage to the airplane, and designated by the airport authorities for use in decelerating the airplane during an aborted takeoff.

Takeoff power—

(1) With respect to reciprocating engines, means the brake horsepower that is developed under standard sea level conditions, and under the maximum conditions of crankshaft rotational speed and engine manifold pressure approved for the normal takeoff, and limited in continuous use to the period of time shown in the approved engine specification; and

(2) With respect to turbine engines, means the brake horsepower that is developed under static conditions at a specified altitude and atmospheric temperature, and under the maximum conditions of rotor shaft rotational speed and gas temperature approved for the normal takeoff, and limited in continuous use to the period of time shown in the approved engine specification.

True airspeed means the airspeed of the aircraft relative to undisturbed air.

Traffic pattern means the traffic flow that is prescribed for aircraft landing at, taxiing on, or taking off from, an airport.

Type—

(1) As used with respect to the certification, ratings, privileges, and

limitations of airmen, means a specific make and basic model of aircraft, including modifications thereto that do not change its handling or flight characteristics. Examples include: DC-7, 1049, and F-27; and

(2) As used with respect to the certification of aircraft, means those aircraft which are similar in design. Examples include: DC-7 and DC-7C, 1049G and 1049H; and F-27 and F-27F.

VFR over-the-top, with respect to the operation of aircraft, means the operation of an aircraft over-the-top under VFR when it is not being operated on an IFR flight plan.

Appendix C

Pilot/Controller Glossary (Abridged)

abbreviated IFR flight plans: An authorization by ATC requiring pilots to submit only that information needed for the purpose of ATC. It includes only a small portion of the usual IFR flight plan information. In certain instances, this be only aircraft identification, location, and pilot request. Other information may be requested if needed by ATC for separation/control purposes. It is frequently used by aircraft which are airborne and desire an instrument approach, or by aircraft which are on the ground and desire a climb to VFR-on-top.

abeam: An aircraft is "abeam" a fix, point, or object when that fix, point, or object is approximately 90 degrees to the right or left of the aircraft track. *Abeam* indicates a general position rather than a precise point.

abort: To terminate a preplanned aircraft maneuver; e.g., an aborted takeoff.

acknowledge: "Let me know that you have received my message."

aerobatic flight: An intentional maneuver involving an abrupt change in an aircraft's attitude, an abnormal attitude, or abnormal acceleration not necessary for normal flight (refer to FAR Part 91). Also called *acrobatic flight.*

additional services: Advisory information provided by ATC which includes but is not limited to the following:

- Traffic advisories.

- Vectors, when requested by the pilot, to assist aircraft receiving traffic advisories to avoid observed traffic.

- Altitude deviation information of 300 feet or more from an assigned altitude as observed on a verified (reading correctly) automatic altitude readout (Mode C).

- Advisories that traffic is no longer a factor.

- Weather and chaff information.

- Weather assistance.

- Bird activity information.

- Holding pattern surveillance.

Additional services are provided to the extent possible contingent only upon the controller's capability to fit them into the performance of higher priority duties and on the basis of the limitations of the radar, volume of traffic, frequency congestion, and controller workload. The controller has complete discretion for determining if he is able to provide or continue to provide a service in a particular case. The controller's reason not to provide a service in a particular case is not subject to question by the pilot and need not be made known to him. (See *Traffic Advisories*.)

Administrator: the Federal Aviation Administrator or any person to whom he has delegated his authority in the matter concerned.

advise intentions: "Tell me what you plan to do."

Advisory: Advice and information provided to assist pilots in the safe conduct of flight and aircraft movement. (See *Advisory Service*.)

Advisory Frequency: The appropriate frequency to be used for Airport Advisory Service. (See *Airport Advisory Service* and *UNICOM*.) Also refer to AC 90-42 and the *Airman's Information Manual*.

Advisory Service: Advice and information provided by a facility to assist pilots in the safe conduct of flight and aircraft movement. (See *Airport Advisory Service, Traffic Advisories, Safety Alerts, additional services, radar advisory,* and *En Route Flight Advisory Service* in *AIM*.)

aeronautical beacon: A visual navaid displaying flashes of white and/or colored light to indicate the location of an airport, a heliport, a landmark, a certain point of a Federal Airway in mountainous terrain, or an obstruction (see *airport rotating beacon*).

aeronautical chart: A map used in air navigation containing all or part of the following: Topographic features, hazards and obstructions, navigation aids, navigation routes, designated airspace, and airports. Commonly used aeronautical charts are:

Sectional Charts—1:500,000—Designed for visual navigation of slow or medium speed aircraft. Topographic information on these charts features the portrayal of relief and a judicious selection of visual check points for VFR flight. Aeronautical information includes visual and radio aids to navigation, airports, controlled airspace, restricted areas, obstructions, and related data.

VFR Terminal Area Charts—1:250,000—Depict Terminal Control Area (TCA) airspace which provides for the control or segregation of all the aircraft within the TCA. The chart depicts topographic information and aeronautical information which includes visual and radio aids to navigation, airports, controlled airspace, restricted areas, obstructions, and related data.

World Aeronautical Charts (WAC)—1:1,000,000—Provide a standard series of aeronautical charts covering land areas of the world at a size and scale convenient for navigation by moderate speed aircraft. Topographic information includes cities, towns, principal roads, railroads, distinctive landmarks, drainage, and relief. Aeronautical information includes visual and radio aids to navigation, airports, airways, restricted areas, obstructions, and other pertinent data.

En Route Low Altitude Charts—Provide aeronautical information for en route instrument navigation (IFR) in the low altitude stratum. Information includes the portrayal of airways, limits of controlled airspace, position identification and radio aid frequencies, selected airports, minimum en route and minimum obstruction clearance altitudes, airway distances, reporting points, restricted areas and related data. Area charts, which are a part of this series, furnish terminal data at a larger scale in congested areas.

En Route High Altitude Charts—Provide aeronautical information for en route instrument navigation (IFR) in the high altitude stratum. Information includes the portrayal of jet routes, identification and frequencies of radio aids, selected airports, distances, time zones, special use airspace, and related information.

Instrument Approach Procedures (IAP) Charts—Portray the aeronautical data that is required to execute an instrument approach to an airport. These charts depict the procedures, including all related data, and the airport diagram. Each procedure is designated for use with a specific type of electronic navigation system, including NDB, TACAN, VOR, ILS/MLS, and RNAV. These charts are identified by the type of navigational aid(s) that provide final approach guidance.

Standard Instrument Departure (SID) Charts—Designed to expedite clearance delivery and to facilitate transition between takeoff and en route operations. Each SID procedure is presented as a separate chart and may serve a single airport or more than one airport in a given geographical location.

Standard Terminal Arrival (STAR) Charts—Designed to expedite air traffic control arrival procedures and to facilitate transition between en route and instrument approach operations. Each STAR procedure is presented as a separate chart and may serve a single airport or more than one airport in a given geographical location.

Airport Taxi Charts—Designed to expedite the efficient and safe flow of ground traffic at an airport. These charts are identified by the official airport name; e.g., Washington National Airport.

affirmative: "Yes."

Aircraft Approach Category: A grouping of aircraft based on a speed of 1.3 times the stall speed in landing configuration at maximum gross landing weight. An aircraft shall fit in only one category. If it is necessary to maneuver at speeds in excess of the upper limit of a speed range for a category, the minimums for the next higher category should be used. For example, an aircraft that falls in Category A, but is circling to land at a speed in excess of 91 knots, should use the approach Category B minimums. The categories are as follows:

- Category A—Speed less than 91 knots.

- Category B—Speed 91 knots or more, but less than 121 knots.

- Category C—Speed 121 knots or more but less than 141 knots.

- Category D—Speed 141 knots or more but less than 166 knots.

- Category E—Speed 166 knots or more (refer to Parts 1 and 97).

Aircraft Classes—For the purposes of wake turbulence separation minima, ATC classifies aircraft as Heavy, Large, and Small, as follows:

Heavy—Aircraft capable of takeoff weights of 300,000 pounds or more, whether or not they are operating at that weight during a particular phase of flight.

Large—Aircraft of more than 12,500 pounds, maximum, certificated takeoff weight, up to 300,000 pounds.

Small—Aircraft of 12,500 pounds or less maximum certificated take-off weight.

Air Defense Identification Zone (ADIZ): The area of airspace over land or water, extending upward from the surface, within which the ready identification, the location, and control of aircraft are required in the interest of national security:

Domestic Air Defense Identification Zone—An ADIZ within the United States along an international boundary of the U.S.

Coastal Air Defense Identification Zone—An ADIZ over the coastal waters of the U.S.

Distant Early Warning Identification Zone (DEWIZ)—An ADIZ over the coastal waters of the State of Alaska.

ADIZ locations and operating and flight plan requirements for civil aircraft operations are specified in FAR Part 99 (See *AIM*).

Airman's Information Manual/AIM: A primary FAA publication whose purpose is to instruct airmen about operating in the National Airspace System of the U.S. It provides basic flight information, ATC Procedures and general instructional information concerning health, medical facts, factors affecting flight safety, accident and hazard reporting, and types of aeronautical charts and their use.

AIRMET (Airman's Meteorological Information): In-flight weather advisories issued only to amend the area forecast concerning weather phenomena which are of operational interest to all aircraft and potentially hazardous to aircraft having limited capability because of lack of equipment, instrumentation, or pilot qualifications. AIRMETs concern weather of less severity than that covered by SIGMETs or Convective SIGMETs. AIRMETs cover moderate icing, moderate turbulence, sustained winds of 30 knots or more at the surface, widespread areas of ceilings less than 1,000 feet and/or visibility less than three miles, and extensive mountain obscurement.

Air Navigation Facility: Any facility used in, available for use in, or designed for use in, aid of air navigation, including landing areas, lights, any apparatus or equipment for disseminating weather information, for signaling, for radio-directional finding, or for radio or other electrical communication, and any other structure or mechanism having a similar purpose for guiding or controlling flight in the air or the landing and take-off of aircraft (see *navigational aid*).

Airport Advisory Area: The area within 10 miles of an airport without a control tower or where the tower is not in operation, and on which a Flight Service Station is located (see *Airport Advisory Service.*)

Airport Advisory Service (AAS): A service provided by Flight Service stations located at airports not serviced by a control tower. This service consists of providing information to arriving and departing aircraft concerning wind direction and speed, favored runway, altimeter setting, pertinent known traffic, pertinent known field conditions, airport taxi routes and traffic patterns, and authorized instrument approach procedures. This information is advisory in nature and does not constitute an ATC clearance.

airport elevation (field elevation): The highest point of an airport's usable runways measured in feet from mean sea level.

Airport/Facility Directory: A publication designed primarily as a pilot's operational manual containing all airports, seaplane bases, and heliports open to the public, including communications data, navigational facilities, and certain special notices and procedures. This publication is issued by the Superintendent of Documents in seven volumes according to geographical area.

Airport Information Desk/AID: An airport unmanned facility designed for pilot self-service briefing, flight planning, and filing of flight plans.

airport lighting: Various lighting aids that may be installed on an airport:

Approach Light System (ALS)—an airport lighting facility that provides visual guidance to landing aircraft by radiating light beams in a directional pattern by which the pilot aligns the aircraft with the extended centerline of the runway on his final approach for landing.

Condenser-discharge sequenced flashing lights may be installed in conjunction with the ALS at some airports. Types of approach light systems are:

- ALSF-1—Approach light system with sequenced flashing lights in ILS Cat-I configuration.

- ALSF-2—Approach light system with sequenced flashing lights in ILS Cat-II configuration. The ALSF-2 may operate as an SSALR when weather conditions permit (see Appendix A).

- SSALF—Simplified short approach light system with sequenced flashing lights.

- SSALR—Simplified short approach light system with runway alignment indicator lights.

- MALSF—Medium intensity approach light system with sequenced flashing lights.

- MALSR—Medium intensity approach light system with runway alignment indicator lights.

- LDIN—Sequenced flashing lead-in lights.

- RAIL—Runway alignment indicator lights (sequenced flashing lights which are installed only in combination with other light systems).

- ODALS—Omnidirectional approach lighting system consists of seven omnidirectional flashing lights located in the approach area of a nonprecision runway. Five lights are located on the runway centerline extended, with the first light 300 feet from the threshold, and extending at equal intervals up to 1,500 feet from the threshold. The other two lights are located, one on each side of the threshold, at a lateral distance of 40 feet from the runway edge, or 75 feet from runway edge when VASI is installed.

Runway lights (runway edge lights)—Lights having a prescribed angle of emission used to define the lateral limits of a runway. Runway lights are uniformly spaced at intervals of approximately 200 feet, and the intensity may be controlled or preset.

Touchdown zone lighting—Two rows of transverse light bars located symmetrically about the runway centerline normally at 100-feet intervals. The basic system extends 3,000 feet along the runway.

Runway centerline lighting—Flush centerline lights at 50-foot intervals beginning 75 feet from the landing threshold and extending to within 75 feet of the opposite end of the runway.

Threshold lights—Fixed green lights arranged symmetrically left and right of the runway centerline, identifying the runway threshold.

Runway End Identifier Lights (REIL)—Two synchronized flashing lights, one on each side of the runway threshold, which provide rapid and positive identification of the approach end of a particular runway.

Visual Approach Slope Indicator (VASI)—An airport lighting facility providing vertical visual approach slope guidance to aircraft during approach to landing by radiating a directional pattern of high intensity red and white focused light beams which indicate to the pilot that he is "on path" if he sees red/white, "above path" if white/white, and "below path" if red/red. Some airports serving large and heavy aircraft have three-bar VASIs, which provide two visual glide paths to the same runway.

Boundary lights—Lights defining the perimeter of an airport or landing area.

airport marking aids: Markings used on runway and taxiway surfaces to identify a specific runway, a runway threshold, a centerline, a hold line, etc. A runway should be marked in accordance with its present usage, such as:

- Visual.

- Nonprecision instrument.

- Precision instrument.

Airport Radar Service Area (ARSA): See *Controlled Airspace.*

airport rotating beacon: A visual navaid operated at many airports. At civil airports, alternating white and green flashes indicate the location of the airport. At military airports, the beacons flash alternately white and green, but the sequence is two quick white flashes between the green flashes.

Airport Service Detection Equipment (ASDE): Radar equipment specifically designed to detect all principal features on the surface of the airport, including aircraft and vehicular traffic, and to present the entire image on a radar indicator console in the control tower. Used to augment visual observation by tower personnel of aircraft and/or vehicular movements on runways and taxiways.

Airport Surveillance Radar (ASR): Approach control radar used to detect and display an aircraft's position in the terminal area. ASR provides range and azimuth information but does not provide elevation data. Coverage of the ASR can extend up to 60 miles.

Airport Traffic Area: Unless otherwise specifically designated in FAR Part 93, that airspace within a horizontal radius of five statue miles from the geographical center of any airport at which a control tower is operating, extending from the surface up to, but not including, an altitude of 3,000 feet above the elevation of an airport. Unless otherwise authorized or required by ATC, no person may operate an aircraft within an airport traffic area except for the purpose of landing at or taking off from an airport within that area. ATC authorization may be given as individual approval of specific operations or may be contained in written agreements between airport users and the tower concerned.

Airport Traffic Control Service: A service provided by a control tower for aircraft operating on the movement area and in the vicinity of an airport (see Movement Area, Tower).

Air Route Surveillance Radar (ARSR): Air route traffic control center (ARTCC) radar used primarily to detect and display an aircraft's position while en route between terminal areas. The ARSR enables controllers to provide radar air traffic control service when aircraft are within the ARSR coverage. In some instances, ARSR may enable an ARTCC to provide terminal radar services similar to but usually more limited than those provided by a radar approach control.

Air Route Traffic Control Center (ARTCC): A facility established to provide air traffic control service to aircraft operating on IFR flight plans within controlled airspace and principally during the en route phase of flight. When equipment capabilities and controller workload permit, certain advisory and assistance services may be provided to VFR aircraft (See *NAS Stage A, En Route Air Traffic Control Service*).

airspeed: The speed of an aircraft relative to its surrounding air mass. The unqualified term *airspeed* means one of the following:

- *Indicated airspeed*—The speed shown on the aircraft airspeed indicator. This is the speed used in pilot/controller communications under the general term *airspeed* (see FAR Part 1).

- True airspeed—The airspeed of an aircraft relative to undisturbed air. Used primarily in flight planning and the en route portion of the flight. When used in pilot/controller communications, it is referred to as *true airspeed* and not shortened to *airspeed.*

air taxi: Used to describe a helicopter or VTOL aircraft movement conducted above the surface but normally not above 100 feet AGL. The aircraft may proceed via hover taxi or flight at speeds more than 20 knots. The pilot is solely responsible for selecting a safe airspeed/altitude for the operation being conducted.

air traffic: Aircraft operating in the air or on an airport surface, exclusive of loading ramps and parking areas.

Air traffic clearance (ATC Clearance): An authorization by Air Traffic Control, for the purpose of preventing collision between known aircraft, for an aircraft to proceed under specified traffic conditions within controlled airspace (see *ATC instructions*).

Air Traffic Control (ATC): A service operated by appropriate authority to promote the safe, orderly and expeditious flow of air traffic.

Air Traffic Control Command Center (ATCCC): An Air Traffic Operations Service facility consisting of four operational units:

- *Central Flow Control Function (CFCF)*—Responsible for coordination and approval of all major intercenter flow control restrictions on a system basis in order to obtain maximum utilization of the airspace . . .

- *Central Altitude Reservation Function (CARF)*—Responsible for coordinating, planning, and approving special user requirements under the Altitude Reservation (ALTRV) concept (see *Altitude Reservation*).

- *Airport Reservation Office (ARO)*—Responsible for approving IFR flight plans at designated high density traffic airports (John F. Kennedy, LaGuardia, O'Hare, and Washington National) during specified hours (refer to FAR Part 93, and *Airport/Facility Directory*).

- *ATC Contingency Command Post*—A facility that enables the FAA to manage the ATC system when significant portions of the system's capabilities have been lost or are threatened.

Air Traffic Control Specialist/Controller: A person authorized to provide Air Traffic Control service (also see *Flight Service Station*).

airway beacon: Used to mark airway segments in remote mountain areas. The light flashes Morse Code to identify the beacon site.

airway (Federal Airway): A control area or portion thereof established in the form of a corridor, the centerline of which is defined by radio navigational aids (refer to FAR Part 71).

Alert Area: See *Special Use Airspace.*

Alert Notice (ALNOT)): A message sent by a Flight Service Station (FSS) or an Air Route Traffic Control Center (ARTCC) that requests an extensive communications search for overdue, unreported, or missing aircraft.

alphanumeric display (data block): Letters and numerals used to show identification, altitude, beacon code, and other information concerning a target on a radar display (see *Automated Radar Terminal Systems, NAS Stage A*).

alternate airport: An airport at which an aircraft may land if a landing at the intended airport becomes inadvisable.

altimeter setting: The barometric pressure reading used to adjust a pressure altimeter for variations in existing atmospheric pressure or to the standard altimeter setting (29.92 Hg).

altitude: The height of a level, point, or object measured in feet above ground level (AGL) or from mean sea level (MSL). Also see *Flight Level.*

- MSL altitude—Altitude expressed in feet measured from mean sea level.

- AGL altitude—Altitude expressed in feet measured above ground level.

- Indicated altitude—The altitude as shown by an altimeter. On a pressure or barometric altimeter it is altitude as shown uncorrected for instrument error and uncompensated for variation from standard atmospheric conditions.

altitude readout (Automatic Altitude Report): An aircraft's altitude, transmitted via the Mode C transponder feature, that is visually displayed in 100-foot increments on a radar scope having readout capability. (See *Automated Radar Terminal Systems, NAS Stage A, alphanumeric display*).

Altitude Reservation (ALTRV): Airspace utilization under prescribed conditions normally employed for the mass movement of aircraft or other special user requirements which cannot otherwise be accomplished. ALTRVs are approved by the appropriate FAA facility.

Altitude Restriction: An altitude or altitudes, stated in the order flown, which are to be maintained until reaching a specific point or time. Altitude restrictions may be issued by ATC due to traffic, terrain, or other airspace considerations.

Altitude Restrictions are cancelled: "Adherence to previously imposed altitude restrictions is no longer required (during a climb or descent."

Approach Clearance: Authorization by ATC for a pilot to conduct an instrument approach. The type of instrument approach for which a clearance and other pertinent information is provided in the approach clearance when required. (See *Approach Control Service, Radar Approach Control Facility.*)

Approach Control Service: Air Traffic Control service provided by an Approach Control facility for arriving and departing VFR/IFR aircraft and, on occasion, en route aircraft. At some airports not served by an Approach Control facility, the ARTCC provides limited Approach Control service.

approach gate: An imaginary point used within ATC as a basis for vectoring aircraft to the final approach course. The gate will be established along the final approach course one mile from the outer marker (or the fix used in lieu of the outer marker) on the side away from the airport for precision approaches, and one miles from the final approach fix on the side away from the airport for nonprecision approaches. In either case, when measured along the final approach course, the gate will be no closer than five miles from the landing threshold.

approach sequence: The order in which aircraft are positioned while on approach or awaiting approach clearance.

approach speed: The recommended speeds contained in aircraft owner's manuals used by pilots when making an approach to land. This speed will vary for different segments of an approach as well as for aircraft weight and configuration.

Area Navigation (RNAV): A method of navigation that permits aircraft operation on any desired course within the coverage of station-referenced navigation signals or within the limits of a self-contained system capability. Random Area Navigation routes are direct routes, based on area navigation capability, between waypoints defined in terms of latitude/longitude coordinates, degree/distance fixes, or offsets from published or established routes/airways at a specified distance and direction. The major types of equipment are:

- *VORTAC referenced* or *Course Line Computer (CLC)* systems, which account for the greatest number of RNAV units in use. To function, the CLC must be within the service range of a VORTAC.

- *OMEGA/VLF,* although two separate systems, can be considered as one operationally. A long-range navigation system based upon Very Low Frequency radio signals transmitted from a total of 17 stations worldwide.

- *Inertial (INS) systems,* which are totally self-contained and require no information from external references. They provide aircraft position and navigation information in response to signals resulting from inertial effects on components within the system.

- *MLS Area Navigation (MLS/RNAV),* which provides area navigation with reference to an MLS ground facility. Random Area Navigation routes are direct routes, based on area navigation capability; see *Area Navigation (RNAV).*

- *Loran-C* is a long-range radio navigation system that uses waves transmitted at low frequency to provide user position information at ranges of up to 600 to 1,200 nautical miles at both en route and approach altitudes. The usable signal coverage areas are determined by the signal-to-noise ratio, the envelope-to-cycle difference, and the geometric relationship between the positions of the user and the transmitting stations.

ARTCC: See *Air Route Traffic Control Center.*
ASR approach: See *Surveillance Approach.*
ATC advises: Used to prefix a message of non-control information when it is relayed to an aircraft by other than an air traffic controller.
ATC Assigned Airspace (ATCAA): Airspace of defined vertical and lateral limits, assigned by ATC for the purpose of providing air traffic segregation between specified activities being conducted within the assigned airspace and other IFR traffic (see *Military Operations Area; Alert Area*).
ATC clears: Used to prefix an ATC clearance when it is relayed to an aircraft by other than an Air Traffic Controller.
ATC instructions: Directives issued by Air Traffic Control for the

purpose of requiring a pilot to take specific actions; e.g., "Turn left heading two five zero." (Refer to FAR Part 91.)

ATCRBS: See *radar.*

ATC requests: Used by other than an Air Traffic Controller to relay an ATC request.

Automated Radar Terminal Systems (ARTS): The generic term for the ultimate in functional capability afforded by several automation systems. Each differs in capability and equipment. ARTS plus a suffix Roman numeral denotes a specific system. In general, an ARTS displays for a terminal controller aircraft identification, flight plan data, other information; e.g., altitude, speed, and aircraft position symbols in conjunction with his radar presentation.

Automatic Altitude Reporting: That function of a transponder that responds to Mode C interrogations by transmitting the aircraft's altitude in 100-foot increments.

Automatic Direction Finder (ADF): An aircraft radio navigation system that senses and indicates the direction to a L/MF nondirectional radio beacon (NDB) ground transmitter. Direction is indicated to the pilot as a magnetic bearing or as a relative bearing to the longitudinal axis of the aircraft, depending upon the type of indicator installed in the aircraft.

Automatic Terminal Information Service (ATIS): The continuous broadcast of recorded non-control information in selected (busy) terminal areas. Its purpose is to improve controller effectiveness and to relieve frequency congestion by automating the repetitive transmission of essential but routine information. (See *AIM.*)

Aviation Weather Service: A service provided by the National Weather Service (NWS) and FAA which collects and disseminates pertinent weather information for pilots and ATC. These reports and forecasts are displayed at each NWS office and FSS (see *En Route Flight Advisory Service, Transcribed Weather Broadcast, Weather Advisory,* and *Pilot's Automatic Telephone Weather Answering Service*).

azimuth, MLS: A magnetic bearing extending from an MLS navigation facility. Note: Azimuth bearings are described as magnetic, and referred to as *azimuth* in aviation radio.

base leg: See *traffic pattern*

beacon: See *radar, nondirectional beacon, marker beacon, airport rotating beacon, aeronautical beacon,* and *airway beacon.*

bearing: The horizontal direction to or from any point, usually measured clockwise from true north, magnetic north, or some other reference point through 360 degrees.

below minimums: Weather conditions below the minimum prescribed by regulation for the particular action involved; e.g., landing minimums and takeoff minimums.

blind spot (blind zone): An area from which radio transmissions and/or radar echoes cannot be received. The term is also used to describe portions of the airport not visible from the control tower.

Braking Action Advisories: When tower controllers have received runway braking action reports which include the terms "poor" or "nil," or whenever weather conditions are conducive to deteriorating or rapidly changing runway braking conditions, the tower will include in the ATIS broadcast the statement, "Braking Action Advisories are in effect," and provide particulars to each arriving and departing aircraft.

call up: Initial voice contact between a facility and an aircraft, using the identification of the unit being called and the unit initiating the call.

Cardinal Altitudes or **Flight Levels:** "Odd" or "even" thousand-foot altitudes or flight levels; e.g., 5,000, 6,000, 7,000, FL 250, FL 260, etc.

ceiling: The heights above the Earth's surface of the lowest layer of clouds or obscuring phenomena that is reported as "broken," "overcast," or "obscuration," and is not classified as "thin" or "partial."

Center: See *Air Route Traffic Control Center.*

Center's Area: The specified airspace within which an Air Route Traffic Control Center (ARTCC) provides Air Traffic Control and advisory service.

Center Weather Advisory (CWA): An unscheduled weather advisory issued by Center Weather Service Unit meteorologists for ATC use to alert pilots of existing or anticipated adverse weather within the next two hours. A CWA may modify or redefine a SIGMET.

Charted VFR Flyways: Flight paths recommended to bypass areas heavily traversed by large jets. Compliance is voluntary. VFR Flyway Planning Charts are printed on reverse sides of VFR Terminal Area charts.

Charted Visual Flight Procedure Approach (CVFP): An approach wherein a radar-controlled aircraft on an IFR flight plan, operating in VFR conditions and having an ATC authorization, may proceed to the airport of intended landing via visual landmarks and altitudes depicted on a charted visual flight procedure.

circle-to-land maneuver (circling maneuver): A maneuver initiated by the pilot to align the aircraft with a runway for landing when a straight-in landing from an instrument approach is not possible or is not desirable. This maneuver is made only after ATC authorization has been obtained and the pilot has established required visual reference to the airport.

circle to runway (specified): Used by ATC to inform the pilot that he must circle to land because the runway in use is other than the runway aligned with the instrument approach procedure.

clear air turbulence (CAT): Turbulence encountered in air where no clouds are present. This term is commonly applied to high-level turbulence associated with wind shear. It is often encountered in the vicinity of the jet stream.

clearance: See *Air Traffic Clearance.*

clearance limit: The fix, point, or location to which an aircraft is cleared when issued an air traffic clearance.

clearance void if not off by (time): Used by ATC to advise a pilot that the departure clearance is automatically cancelled if takeoff is not made prior to a specified time. The pilot must obtain a new clearance or cancel his IFR flight plan if not off by the specified time.

cleared as filed: Means the aircraft is cleared to proceed in accordance with the route of flight filed in the flight plan. This clearance does not include the altitude, SID, or SID transition. (See *request full route clearance.*)

cleared for (type of) approach: ATC authorization for an aircraft to execute a specific instrument approach procedure to an airport; e.g., "Cleared for ILS runway three six approach."

cleared for approach: ATC authorization for an aircraft to execute any standard or special instrument approach procedure for that airport. Normally, an aircraft will be cleared for a specific instrument approach procedure.

cleared for takeoff: ATC authorization for an aircraft to depart. It is predicated on known traffic and known physical airport conditions.

cleared for the option: ATC authorization for an aircraft to make a touch-and-go, low approach, missed approach, stop and go, or full stop landing at the discretion of the pilot; normally used in training.

cleared through: ATC authorization for an aircraft to make intermediate stops at specified airports without refiling a flight plan while en route to the clearance limit.

cleared to land: ATC authorization for an aircraft to land. It is predicated on known traffic and known physical airport conditions.

climbout: That portion of flight operation between takeoff and the initial cruising altitude.

climb to VFR: ATC authorization for an aircraft to climb to VFR conditions within a Control Zone when the only weather limitation is restricted visibility. The aircraft must remain clear of clouds while climbing to VFR (see *Special VFR*).

closed traffic: Successive operations involving takeoffs and landings or low approaches where the aircraft does not exit the traffic pattern.

coastal fix: A navigation aid or intersection where an aircraft transitions between the domestic route structure and the oceanic route structure.

codes (transponder codes): The number assigned to a particular multiple pulse reply signal transmitted by a transponder (see *discrete code*).

Combined Center-Rapcon (CERAP): An air traffic facility that combines the functions of ARTCC and a Radar Approach Control Facility.

Common Traffic Advisory Frequency (CTAF): A frequency designed for the purpose of carrying out airport advisory practices while operating to or from an uncontrolled airport. The CTAF may be a

UNICOM, Multicom, FSS, or tower frequency, and is identified in appropriate aeronautical publications (refer to AC 90-42D).

compass locator: A low-power, low or medium-frequency (L/MF) radio beacon installed at the site of the outer or middle marker of an instrument landing system (ILS). It can be used for navigation at distances of approximately 15 miles or as authorized in the approach procedure.

- Outer compass locator (LOM)—A compass locator installed at the site of the outer marker of an ILS.

- Middle compass locator (LMM)—A compass locator installed at the site of the middle marker of an ILS.

compass rose: A circle, graduated in degrees, printed on some charts or marked on the ground at an airport. It is used as a reference to either true or magnetic direction.

compulsory reporting points: Reporting points that must be reported to ATC. They are designated on aeronautical charts by solid triangles, or filed in a flight plan as fixes selected to define direct routes. These points are geographical locations that are defined by navigation aids/fixes. Pilots should discontinue position reporting over compulsory reporting points when informed by ATC that their aircraft is in radar contact.

Conflict Alert: A function of certain ATC automated systems designed to alert a radar controller to existing or pending situations that require his immediate attention/action.

Consolan: A low-frequency, long-distance Navaid used principally for transoceanic navigation.

contact:

- "Establish communication with (followed by the name of the facility and, if appropriate, the frequency to be used)."

- A flight condition wherein the pilot ascertains the attitude of his aircraft and navigates by visual reference to the surface.

contact approach: An approach wherein an aircraft on an IFR flight plan, with ATC authorization, operating clear of clouds with at least one mile flight visibility, and a reasonable expectation of continuing to the destination airport in those conditions, may deviate from the instrument approach procedure and proceed to the airport by visual reference to the surface. This approach will be authorized only when requested by the pilot, and when reported ground visibility at the airport is at least one mile.

conterminous U.S.—The 48 adjoining states and the District of Columbia.

Continental Control Area: See *Controlled Airspace.*

continental U.S.: The 49 states located on the continent of North America and the District of Columbia.

Control Area: See *Controlled Airspace.*

Controlled Airspace: Airspace designated as a Control Zone, Airport Radar Service Area, Terminal Control Area, Transition Area, Control Area, Continental Control Area, and Positive Control Area within which some or all aircraft may be subject to air traffic control (FAR Part 71).

Control Zone—Controlled airspace that extends upward from the surface of the earth and terminates at the base of the Continental Control Area. Control Zones that do not underlie the Continental Control Area have no upper limit. A Control Zone may include one or more airports and is normally a circular area with a radius of five statute miles, and any extension necessary to include instrument approach and departure paths.

Airport Radar Service Area (ARSA)—Regulatory airspace surrounding designated airports wherein ATC provides radar vectoring and sequencing on a fulltime basis for all IFR and VFR aircraft. The service provided in an ARSA includes: IFR separation; IFR/VFR traffic advisories and conflict resolution; VFR traffic advisories and, as appropriate, safety alerts. ARSAs are shown on VFR aeronautical charts. (See FAR Part 91; *Airport/Facility Directory.*)

Terminal Control Area (TCA)—Controlled airspace extending upward from the surface or higher to specified altitudes, within which all aircraft are subject to operating rules and pilot and equipment requirements specified in FAR Part 91. TCAs are shown on Sectional, WAC, En Route Low Altitude, DOD FLIP, and TCA charts.

Transition Area—Controlled airspace extending upward from 700 feet or more above the surface when designated in conjunction with an airport for which an approved instrument approach procedure has been prescribed, or from 1,200 feet or more above the surface when designated in conjunction with airway route structures or segments. Unless otherwise specified, Transition Areas terminate at the base of the overlying controlled airspace. Transition areas are designed to contain IFR operations in controlled airspace in portions of the terminal operation, and while transiting between the terminal and the en route environment.

Control Area—Airspace designed as Colored Federal Airways, VOR Federal Airways, Control Areas associated with jet routes outside the continental control area (FAR 71.161), additional Control Areas (FAR 71.163), Control Area extensions (FAR 71.165), and Area Low Routes. Control Areas do not include the Continental Control area, but unless otherwise designated, they do include the airspace between a segment of a main VOR Federal Airway and its associated alternate segments, with the vertical extent of the area corresponding to the vertical extent of the related segment of the main airway. Vertical limits are defined in FAR Part 71.

Continental Control Area—The airspace of the 48 contiguous states, the District of Columbia and Alaska, excluding the Alaska peninsula west of Long. 160 degrees and 00 minutes 00 seconds W., at and above 14,500 ft MSL, but does not include:

- The airspace less than 1,500 feet above the surface, or

- Prohibited and restricted areas, other than the restricted areas listed in FAR Part 71.

Positive Control Area (PCA)—Airspace designated in FAR Part 71 within which there is positive control of aircraft. Flight in PCA is normally conducted IFR. PCA is designated throughout most of the conterminous U.S., and its vertical extent is from 18,000 feet MSL to and including Flight Level 600 (60,000 feet). In Alaska, PCA does not include the airspace less than 1,500 feet above the surface, or the airspace over the Alaskan Peninsula west of longitude 160 degrees W. (See FAR Part 91.97 and 91.24)

Controlled Departure Time (CDT): The flow control process whereby aircraft are held on the ground at the departure airport when delays are projected to occur in either the en route system or the terminal of intended landing. A CDT is a specific departure slot shown on the flight plan as an expected departure clearance time (EDCT).

controller: See *Air Traffic Control Specialist.*

Control Sector: A block of airspace normally controlled by Center or Approach Control. Sectors are established based on predominant traffic flows and controller workload. Communications are normally via discrete frequencies (see *discrete frequency*).

Convective SIGMET: A weather advisory concerning convective weather significant to the safety of all aircraft. Convective SIGMETs are issued for tornados, lines of thunderstorms, embedded thunderstorms of any intensity level, areas of thunderstorms greater than or equal to VIP Level 4 with an area coverage of $\frac{4}{10}$ (40%) or more, and hail ¾ inch or greater. (See *SIGMET, CWA,* and *AIRMET.*)

coordinates:—The intersection of lines of reference, usually expressed in degrees/minutes/seconds of longitude and latitude; used to determine position or location.

coordination fix: The fix in relation to which facilities will hand off, transfer control of an aircraft, or coordinate flight progress data. For terminal facilities, it may also serve as a clearance for arriving aircraft.

course:

- The intended direction of flight in the horizontal plane measured is degrees from north.

- The ILS localizer signal pattern usually specified as the front course or the back course.

- The intended track along a straight, curved, or segmented MLS path. (See *bearing*.)

critical engine: The engine which, upon failure, would most adversely affect the performance or handling qualities of an aircraft.
crosswind:

- When used concerning the traffic pattern, it means "crosswind leg."

- When used concerning wind conditions, it means a wind not parallel to the runway or the path of an aircraft.

crosswind component: The wind component measured in knots at 90 degrees to the longitudinal axis of the runway.
cruise: Used in an ATC clearance to authorize a pilot to conduct flight at any altitude from the minimum IFR altitude up to and including the altitude specified in the clearance. The pilot may level off at any intermediate altitude within this block of airspace. Climb/descent with the block is to be made at the discretion of the pilot. However, once the pilot starts descent and verbally reports leaving an altitude in the block, he may not return to that altitude without additional ATC clearance. Further, it is approval for the pilot to proceed to and make an approach at his destination airport, and can be used in conjunction with:

- An airport clearance limit at locations with an instrument approach procedure.

- An airport clearance limit at locations that are within, below, or outside controlled airspace and without a standard/special instrument approach procedure. Such a clearance is not authorization for descent below applicable IFR minimums, and does not imply ATC control in uncontrolled airspace. It provides a means to proceed to the destination airport, descend, and land in accordance with VFR procedures. (See *Instrument Approach Procedure*.)

cruising altitude (level): An altitude or flight level maintained during en route level flight. This is a constant altitude and should not be confused with a cruise clearance.

decision height (DH): The height at which a decision must be made during an ILS, MLS, or PAR instrument approach to either continue or execute a missed approach.
Defense Visual Flight Rules (DVFR): Rules applicable to flight within an ADIZ conducted under the visual flight rules in FAR Part 91.
Departure Control: A function of an Approach Control facility

providing Air Traffic Control service for departing IFR and, under certain conditions, VFR aircraft.

departure time: The time an aircraft becomes airborne.

DF approach: DF guidance for an instrument approach may be given by ATC with DF capability when another instrument approach cannot be made.

DF fix: The geographical location of an aircraft obtained by one or more direction finders.

DF guidance (DF steer): Headings provided to aircraft by facilities equipped with DF equipment. Direction finding guidance is given to aircraft in distress (lost) and for practice when flight specialist's workload permits.

direct: Straight-line flight between two navigational aids, fixes, points, or any combination thereof. When used in describing off-airway routes, points defining direct route segments become compulsory reporting points unless the aircraft is in radar contact.

direction finder (DF): A radio receiver equipped with a directional sensing antenna used to take bearings on a radio transmitter. Specialized radio direction finders are used in aircraft as air navigation aids. Others are group-based, primarily to obtain a fix on a pilot requesting orientation assistance or to locate downed aircraft.

discrete code: As used in the ATC Radar Beacon System (ATCRBS), any one of the 4096 selectable Mode 3/A aircraft transponder codes, except those ending in zero-zero.

discrete frequency: A separate radio frequency for use in direct pilot-controller communications in Air Traffic Control which reduces frequency congestion by controlling the number of aircraft operating on a particular frequency at one time.

displaced threshold: A threshold that is located at a point on the runway other than the designated beginning of the runway.

Distance Measuring Equipment (DME): Equipment (airborne and ground) used to measure, in nautical miles, the slant range distance of an aircraft from the DME navigational aid.

DME fix: A geographical position determined by reference to a navigational aid which provides distance and azimuth information. It is defined by a specific distance in nautical miles and a radial, azimuth, or course (i.e., localizer) in degrees magnetic from that aid.

downwind leg: See *traffic pattern.*

Emergency Locator Transmitter (ELT): A radio transmitter attached to the aircraft structure which operates from its own power source on 121.5 MHz and 243.0 MHz as an aid in locating downed aircraft by radiating a distinctive audio tone.

En Route Flight Advisory Service (Flight Watch): A service specifically designed to provide, upon pilot request, timely weather information pertinent to his type of flight, intended route of flight, and altitude. The FSSs providing this type of service are listed in the *Airport/Facility Directory.*

execute missed approach: Instructions issued to a pilot making an instrument approach which means continue inbound to the missed approach point and execute the missed approach procedure as described on the Instrument Approach Procedure Chart, or as previously assigned by ATC. When conducting an ASR or PAR approach, execute the missed approach procedure immediately upon receiving the ATC instruction.

expected departure clearance time (EDCT): The runway release time assigned to an aircraft in a controlled departure time program (flow control), and shown on the flight progress strip as an EDCT.

expedite: Used by ATC when prompt compliance is essential.

fast file: A system whereby a pilot files a flight plan via telephone that is taped and then transcribed for transmission to the appropriate ATC facility. Locations with fast file capability are listed in the *Airport/Facility Directory.*

feathered propeller: A propeller whose blades have been rotated so that the leading and trailing edges are nearly parallel with the aircraft flight path to minimize drag and stop rotation of an inoperative engine.

feeder route: A route depicted on approach (instrument) procedure charts connecting the en route structure with the initial approach fix. See *Instrument Approach Procedure.*

filed: Normally used in conjunction with flight plans, meaning that a flight plan has been submitted to ATC.

final: Commonly used to mean that an aircraft is on the final approach course or is aligned with a landing area.

final approach course: A published MLS course, a straight line extension of a localizer, a final approach radial/bearing, or a runway centerline, all without regard to distance.

final approach fix (FAF): The fix from which the final approach (IFR) to an airport is executed and which identifies the beginning of the final approach segment. It is shown on the charts as a Maltese Cross symbol for nonprecision approaches, and by a lightning bolt symbol for precision approaches.

final approach point (FAP): The point, applicable only to a nonprecision approach with no depicted FAF (such as an on-airport VOR), where the aircraft is established on the final approach course from the procedure turn and where the final approach descent may be started. The FAP serves as the FAF and identifies the beginning of the final approach segment.

fix: A geographical position determined by visual reference to the surface, by reference to one or more radio navaids, or by other navigational device or procedure.

flight level: A level of constant atmospheric pressure related to a reference datum of 29.92 inches of mercury. Each is stated in three digits that represents hundreds of feet, e.g., flight level 250 indicates a barometric altimeter reading of 25,000 feet.

flight path: A line, course, or track along which an aircraft is flying or intended to be flown.

flight plan: Specified information relating to the intended flight of an aircraft that is filed orally or in writing with an FSS or an ATC facility.

Flight Service Station (FSS): Air traffic facilities that provide pilot briefing, en route communications and VFR search and rescue services; assist lost aircraft, and aircraft in distress; relay ATC clearances; originate Notices to Airmen, broadcast aviation weather and NAS information; receive and process IFR flight plans; and monitor navaids. In addition, at selected locations, FSSs provide en route Flight Advisory Service (Flight Watch), take weather observations, issue airport advisories, and advise Customs and Immigration of trans-border flights.

Flight Standards District Office (FSDO) [pronounced "fisdo"]: An FAA field office serving an assigned geographical area and staffed with Flight Standards personnel who serve the industry and the general public on matters relating to the certification and operation of air carrier and general aviation aircraft.

Flight Watch: A shortened term for use in air-ground contacts on frequency 122.0 MHz to identify the FAA providing En Route Flight Advisory Service.

flow control: Measure designed to adjust the flow of traffic into a given airspace, along a given route, or bound for a given airport, so as to ensure the most effective utilization of the airspace.

gate hold procedures: Procedures at selected airports to hold aircraft at the gate or other ground location whenever departure delays exceed or are anticipated to exceed 15 minutes. The sequence for departure will be maintained in accordance with initial call-up unless modified by flow control restrictions. Pilots should monitor the ground control/clearance delivery frequency for engine startup advisories or new proposed start time if the delay changes.

general aviation: That portion of civil aviation which encompasses all facets of the industry except the airlines.

General Aviation District Office (GADO): An FAA field office serving a designated geographical area and staffed with Flight Standards personnel who have the responsibility for serving the aviation industry and the general public on all matters relating to the certification and operation of general aviation aircraft.

Glideslope: Provides vertical guidance for aircraft during approach and landing and is based on the following:

- Electronic signals which provide guidance by reference to instruments in the airplane.

- Visual ground aids such as VASI.

- Precision Approach Radar (PAR)—Used by ATC to inform aircraft making a PAR approach of its vertical position relative to the descent profile.

glideslope intercept altitude: The minimum altitude to intercept the glideslope on a precision approach.

go ahead: Means "Proceed with your message." Not to be used for any other purpose in ATC communications.

go around: "Abandon your landing approach." Additional instructions may follow. Unless otherwise advised, aircraft conduction a visual approach should overfly the runway while climbing to traffic pattern altitude and enter the pattern on the crosswind leg.

Ground Controlled Approach (GCA): A radar approach system operated from the ground by ATC personnel transmitting instructions to the pilot by radio.

ground speed: The speed of an aircraft relative to the surface of the earth.

handoff: An action taken to transfer the radar identification of an aircraft from one controller to another.

have numbers: Used by pilots to inform ATC that they have received runway, wind, and altimeter information only.

Hazardous Inflight Weather Advisory Service (HIWAS): A program for broadcasting hazardous weather information on a continuous basis over selected VORs.

Heavy Aircraft: See *Aircraft Classes.*

Height Above Airport (HAA): The height of the Minimum Descent Altitude above the published airport elevation. It is published in conjunction with circling minimums.

Height Above Touchdown (HAT): The Decision Height or Minimum Descent Altitude above the highest runway elevation in the touch-down zone (first 3,000 feet of the runway).

Hertz (Hz): The standard radio equivalent of frequency in cycles per second in an electromagnetic wave. Kilohertz (kHz) is a frequency of one thousand cycles per second. Megahertz (MHz) is a frequency of one million cycles per second.

high-frequency (HF): The frequency band between 3 and 30 MHz.

high-speed taxiway: An angled taxiway that allows a high speed exit from the runway after landing, thus reducing runway occupancy time.

holding fix: A specified fix used as a reference while holding and awaiting further clearance from ATC.

homing: Flight toward a navaid, without correcting for wind, by adjusting the aircraft heading to maintain a relative bearing of zero degrees.

ident: A request for a pilot to activate the aircraft transponder identification feature.

IFR: Instrument Flight Rules.

IFR Military Training Routes (IR): Routes used by DoD and Air Guard/Reserve units for the purpose of conducting low-altitude navigation and tactical training in both IFR and VFR conditions below 10,000 feet MSL at airspeeds in excess of 250 knots IAS.

IFR Takeoff Minimums and Departure Procedures: FAR Part 91 prescribes standard takeoff rules.

ILS Categories:

- ILS Category I—An ILS approach procedure that provides for approach to a height above touchdown of not less than 200 feet and with a runway visual range (RVR) of not less than 1,200 feet.

- ILS Category II—An ILS approach procedure that provides for an approach to a height above touchdown of not less than 100 feet and with RVR of not less than 1,200 feet.

- ILS Category IIIA—An ILS approach procedure that provides for approach without a decision height (DH) minimum and with a runway visual range of not less than 700 feet.

- ILS Category IIIB—No decision height minimum, but an RVR of not less than 150 feet.

- ILS Category IIIC—No minimum DH required, and no minimum runway visual range.

Initial Approach Fix (IAF): The fixes depicted on instrument approach procedure charts that identify the beginning of the initial approach segment(s).

inner marker (IM): A marker beacon used with an ILS (CAT II) precision approach located between the middle marker and the end of the ILS runway which indicates the 100-foot DH for CAT II approach.

Instrument Approach Procedure (IAP): A series of predetermined maneuvers for the orderly transfer of an IFR aircraft from the beginning of the initial approach to a landing or to a point from which a landing may be made visually.

- U.S. civil standard instrument approach procedures are approved by the FAA as prescribed under FAR Part 97.

- U.S. military standard instrument approach procedures are approved by the DoD.

- Special instrument approach procedures are approved by the FAA, but are not published in Part 97 for public use.

Instrument Landing System (ILS): A precision instrument approach system which normally consists of a localizer, glideslope, outer marker, middle marker, and approach lights.

instrument runway: A runway equipped with electronic and visual aids for which a precision or nonprecision approach procedure having straight-in landing minimums has been approved.

- Instrument Approach Runway—An instrument runway served by a non-visual aid providing at least directional guidance adequate for a straight-in approach.

- Precision Approach Runway, Category I—An instrument runway served by ILS or GCA and visual aids, approved for CAT I operations. CAT II and CAT IIIs similarly designated.

International Flight Information Manual (IFIM): A publication designed primarily as a pilot's preflight planning guide for flights into foreign airspace, and flights returning to the U.S. from foreign locations.
intersection: A point defined by any combination of courses, radials, or bearings of two or more navaids, or the point where two runways, a runway and a taxiway, or two taxiways cross or meet.

jet route: A route designed to serve aircraft operating from 18,000 feet MSL up to and including FL 450. These are referred to as "J" routes.
jet stream: A migrating stream of high-speed winds present at high altitudes.

landing minimums: The minimum visibility prescribed for landing a civil aircraft using an instrument approach procedure. Refer to Part 91.
landing roll: The distance from the point of touchdown to the point where the aircraft can be brought to a stop or exit the runway.
light gun (biscuit gun): A tower controller's handheld directional signalling device which emits a narrow beam of red, white, or green light; used when radio contact with aircraft is not established.
localizer: The component of an ILS that provides course guidance to the runway.
LORAN (Long Range Navigation): An electronic navigational system by which hyperbolic lines of position are determined by measuring the difference in the time of reception of synchronized pulse signals from two fixed transmitters. LORAN-C operates in the 100 to 110 kHz frequency band.
Low Approach: An approach over an airport or runway following an instrument approach or VFR approach, including the go-around maneuver where the pilot intentionally does not make contact with the runway.
low-frequency (LF): The frequency band between 30 and 300 kHz.

Mach number: The ratio of true airspeed to the speed of sound; e.g., Mach .82, Mach 1.6, etc.
marker beacon: An electronic navigation facility transmitting a 75 MHz vertical fan or bone-shaped radiation pattern.
Mayday: The international radiotelephony distress signal. When

repeated three times, it indicates imminent and grave danger and that immediate assistance is requested. Also, see *Pan-Pan*.

Meteorological Impact Statement (MIS): An unscheduled planning forecast describing conditions expected to begin within four to 12 hours which may impact the flow of air traffic in a specific center's area.

Microwave Landing System (MLS): A precision instrument approach system operating in the microwave spectrum which normally consists of azimuth station, elevation station, and Precision Distance Measuring Equipment.

middle marker (MM): A marker beacon that defines a point along the glideslope of an ILS normally located at or near the point of decision height (ILS Category I).

Military Operations Area (MOA): See *Special Use Airspace*.

Military Training Routes (MTR): A block of airspace established for the conduct of military flight training at airspeeds in excess of 250 knots IAS.

Minimum Crossing Altitude (MCA): The lowest altitude at certain fixes at which an aircraft must cross when proceeding in the direction of a higher minimum en route IFR altitude (MEA).

Minimum Descent Altitude (MDA): The lowest altitude above MSL to which descent is authorized on final approach or during circle-to-land maneuvering in a standard instrument approach where no electronic glideslope is provided.

Minimum En Route IFR Altitude (MEA): The lowest published altitude between radio fixes that assures acceptable navigational signal coverage and also meets obstacle clearance requirements.

Minimum Holding Altitude (MHA): The lowest altitude prescribed for a holding pattern that assures navigational signal coverage, communications, and meets obstacle clearance requirements.

Minimum IFR Altitudes (MIA): Minimum altitudes for IFR operations as prescribed in FAR Part 91. These altitudes are published on aeronautical charts, and prescribed in Part 95 for airways and routes, and in Part 97 for standard instrument approach procedures.

Minimum Obstruction Clearance Altitude (MOCA): The lowest published altitude in effect between radio fixes on VOR airways, off-airway routes, or route segments which meets obstacle clearance requirements, and which assures acceptable nav-signal coverage only within 25 statute miles of a VOR.

Minimum Reception Altitude (MRA): The lowest altitude at which an intersection can be determined.

Minimum Safe Altitude (MSA): The minimum altitude specified in Part 91 for various aircraft operations.

Minimum Vectoring Altitude (MVA): The lowest MSL altitude at which an IFR aircraft will be vectored by a radar controller, except as otherwise authorized for radar approaches, departures, and missed approaches.

missed approach: A maneuver conducted by a pilot when an instrument approach cannot be completed to a landing.

Missed Approach Point (MAP): A point prescribed in each instrument approach procedure at which a missed approach shall be executed if the required visual reference does not exist.

navigational aid (navaid): Any visual or electronic device, airborne or on the surface, that provides point-to-point guidance information or position data to aircraft in flight.

NDB: See *nondirectional beacon.*

negative: "No," or "Permission not granted," or "That is not correct."

negative contact: Used by pilots to inform ATC that: 1) Previously issued traffic is not in sight, and it may be followed by the pilot's request for the controller to provide assistance in avoiding the traffic; and 2) Pilot unable to contact ATC on a particular frequency.

night: The time between the end of evening civil twilight and the beginning of morning civil twilight, as published in the American Air Almanac, converted to local time.

no gyro approach (vector): Radar approach vectors provided by the controller in case of an aircraft's malfunctioning gyro-compass or directional gyro.

Non Approach Control Tower: Authorizes aircraft to land or take off or to transit the airport traffic area. Its primary function is to sequence aircraft in the pattern and on the airport.

nondirectional beacon (NDB): An L/MF or UHF radio beacon transmitting nondirectional signals whereby the pilot of an aircraft equipped with DF equipment can determine his bearing to or from the beacon and "home" on, or track to or from it. When the NDB is installed in conjunction with the ILS marker, it is normally called a "compass locator." (See *Automatic Direction Finder.*)

nonprecision approach: A standard instrument approach procedure in which no electronic glideslope is provided, e.g., VOR, TACAN, NDB, LOC, ASR, LDA, or SDF approaches.

non-radar: Precedes other terms, and generally means without the use of radar, such as:

- Non-radar route—A flight path or route over which the pilot is performing his own navigation, although he may be receiving other ATC services, including radar separation.

- Non-radar approach—Used to describe instrument approaches for which course guidance on final approach is not provided by ground-based precision or surveillance radar. Radar vectors to the final approach course may or may not be provided by ATC.

Notice to Airmen (NOTAM): A notice containing information, not known sufficiently in advance to publicize by other means, concerning the establishment, condition, or change in any component (facility, service, or procedure of, or hazard in the National Airspace System), the timely knowledge of which is essential to personnel concerned with flight operations.

Numerous targets vicinity (with location given): A traffic advisory issued by ATC to advise pilots that targets on the radar scope are too numerous to issue individually.

obstruction: Any object/obstacle exceeding the obstruction standards specified by FAR Part 77, SubPart C.

off-route vector: A vector by ATC that takes an aircraft off of a previously assigned route. Altitudes assigned by ATC during such vectors provide the required obstacle clearance.

offset parallel runways: Staggered runways having centerlines that are parallel.

out: [Used in years past to indicate that] the conversation is ended and no reply is expected.

outer area: As associated with ARSAs: Non-regulatory airspace surrounding designated ARSA airports wherein ATC provides radar vectoring and sequencing on a fulltime basis for all IFR and participating VFR aircraft. The service provided in the outer area is called ARSA Service which includes: IFR/IFR, standard IFR separation; IFR/VFR, traffic advisories and conflict resolution; and VFR/VFR traffic advisories and, as appropriate, safety alerts. The normal radius will be 20 nautical miles, with some variations based on site-specific requirements. The outer area extends outward from the primary ARSA airport and extends from the lower limits of radar/radio coverage up to the ceiling of the Approach Control's delegated airspace, excluding the ARSA and other airspace as appropriate.

outer marker (OM): A marker beacon at or near the glideslope intercept altitude of an ILS approach. It transmits two dashes per second on a 400 Hz tone, and is normally located four to seven miles from the runway threshold on the extended centerline of the runway.

over: "My transmission is ended; I expect a response."

overhead approach (360 overhead): A series of predetermined maneuvers prescribed for VFR arrival of military aircraft.

Pan-Pan: The international radio-telephony urgency signal. When repeated three times, indicates uncertainty or an alert, followed by the nature of the problem. See *Mayday.*

parallel ILS/MLS approaches: Approaches to parallel runways by IFR aircraft which, when established inbound toward the airport on the adjacent final approach courses are radar-separated by at least two miles.

parallel offset route: A parallel track to the left or right of the designated or established airway/route. Normally associated with Area Navigation (RNAV) operations.

parallel runways: Two or more runways at the same airport whose centerlines are parallel. In addition to number, parallel runways are designated as L (left) and R (right).

pilot in command: The pilot responsible for the operation and safety of an aircraft during flight time. See FAR Part 91.

Pilots' Automatic Telephone Weather Answering Service (PATWAS): A continuous telephone recording containing current and forecast weather information for pilots.

pilot's discretion: When used in conjunction with altitude assignments, means that ATC has offered the pilot the option of starting climb or descent whenever he wishes and conducting the climb or descent at any rate he wishes. He may temporarily level off at any intermediate altitude; however, once he has vacated an altitude, he may not return to that altitude without further ATC clearance.

Pilot Weather Report (PIREP): A report of meteorological phenomena encountered in flight.

position report (progress report): A report over a known location transmitted by an aircraft to ATC.

Positive Control: The separation of all air traffic within designated airspace by ATC. See *Positive Control Area* under controlled airspace.

precision approach: A standard instrument approach procedure in which an electronic glideslope/glide path is provided, e.g., ILS/MLS and PAR. See *Instrument Landing System.*

Precision Approach Radar (PAR): Radar equipment in some ATC facilities operated by the FAA and/or the military at joint use civil/military locations to detect and display azimuth, elevation, and range of aircraft on the final approach course to a runway.

Preferred IFR Routes: Routes established between busier airports to increase system efficiency and capacity. They normally extend through one or more ARTCC areas and are designed to achieve balanced traffic flows among high-density terminals. IFR clearances are issued on the basis of these routes except when severe weather avoidance or other factors dictate otherwise.

procedure turn inbound: That point of a procedure turn maneuver where course reversal has been completed and the aircraft is established inbound on the intermediate approach segment or final approach course. A report of "Procedure turn inbound" is normally used by ATC as a position report for separation purposes.

procedure turn (PT): The maneuver prescribed when it is necessary to reverse direction to establish an aircraft on the intermediate approach segment or final approach course. The outbound course, direction of turn, distance within which the turn must be completed, and minimum altitude are specified in the procedure. However, unless otherwise restricted, the point at which the turn may be started, and the type and rate of turn, are left to the discretion of the pilot.

profile descent: An uninterrupted descent (except for level flight required for speed adjustment) from cruising altitude to interception of a glideslope, or to a minimum altitude specified for the initial or intermediate approach segment of a nonprecision instrument approach. The profile descent normally terminates at the approach gate or where the glideslope or other appropriate minimum altitude is intercepted.

quadrant: A quarter part of a circle, centered on a navaid, oriented clockwise from magnetic north as follows: NE quadrant, 000-089 degrees; SE quadrant, 090-179 degrees; SW quadrant, 180-269 degrees, and NW quadrant, 270-359 degrees.

radar (Radio Detection and Ranging): A device which, by measuring the time interval between transmission and reception of radio pulses, and correlating the angular orientation of the radiated antenna beam or beams in azimuth and/or elevation, provides information on range, azimuth, and/or elevation of objects in the path of the transmitted pulses.

Radar Approach Control Facility: A terminal ATC facility that uses radar and non-radar capabilities to provide approach control services to aircraft operating in the vicinity. The facility may provide services of a GCA, ASR, and PAR approaches, and may be operated by FAA, USAF, US Army, USN, USMC, or jointly by FAA and a military service. Two examples are: Radar Approach Control (RAPCON), and Terminal Radar Approach (TRACON).

Radar Weather Echo Intensity Levels: The National Weather Service has categorized six levels of radar weather echo intensity. The levels are sometimes expressed during communications as "VIP Level" one through six (derived from the component of the weather radar that produces the information—Video Integrator and Processor):

- Level 1 (weak) and Level 2 (moderate)—Light to moderate turbulence is possible with lightning.

- Level 3 (strong)—Severe turbulence possible, lightning.

- Level 4 (very strong)—Severe turbulence likely, lightning.

- Level 5 (Intense)—Severe turbulence, lightning, organized wind gusts, hail likely.

- Level 6 (extreme). Severe turbulence, large hail, lightning, and extensive wind gusts.

radial: A magnetic bearing extending from a VOR/VORTAC/TACAN navigation facility.

radio: Used to refer to a Flight Service Station, e.g., "Seattle Radio" is used to call the Seattle FSS.

radio altimeter (radar altimeter): Aircraft equipment that makes use of the reflection of radio waves from the ground to determine the height of the aircraft above the surface.

radio beacon: See *nondirectional beacon, NDB.*

Radio Magnetic Indicator (RMI): An aircraft navigation instrument coupled with a gyro compass or similar compass that indicates the direction of a selected navaid and displays bearing with respect to the heading of the aircraft.

read back: "Repeat my message back to me."

release time: A departure time restriction issued to a pilot by ATC when necessary to separate a departing aircraft from other traffic.

Remote Communications Air-Ground Facility (RCAG): An unmanned VHF/UHF transmitter/receiver facility that is used to expand ARTCC air-ground communications coverage and to facilitate direct contact between pilots and controllers.

Remote Communications Outlet (RCO) and Remote Transmitter and Receiver (RTR): An unmanned communications facility remotely controlled by air traffic personnel. RCOs serve FSS. RTRs serve terminal ATC facilities. These installations were established for the purpose of providing ground-to-ground communications between ATC specialists and pilots located at a satellite airport for delivering en route clearances, issuing departure authorizations, and acknowledging IFR cancellations or departure/landing times. As a secondary function, they may be used for advisory purposes whenever the aircraft is below the coverage of the primary air/ground frequency.

report: Used to instruct pilots to advise ATC of specified information, e.g., "Report passing Hamilton VOR."

reporting point: A geographical location in relation to which the position of an aircraft is reported. See compulsory reporting point.

RNAV: See *Area Navigation.*

roger: "I have received all of your last transmission." It should not be used to answer a question requiring a "yes" or "no" reply (See *affirmative, negative*).

route: A defined path, consisting of one or more courses in a horizontal plane, which aircraft traverse over the surface of the earth.

route segment: As used in air traffic control, a part of a route that can be defined by two navigational fixes, two navaids, or a fix and a navaid.

runway: A defined rectangular area on a land airport prepared for the landing and takeoff run of an aircraft along its length. Runways are numbered in relation to their magnetic direction, rounded off to the nearest 10 degrees, minus the final digit.

Safety Alert: A safety alert issued by ATC to aircraft under their control if ATC is aware the aircraft is at an altitude which, in the controller's judgment, places the aircraft in unsafe proximity to terrain, obstructions, or other aircraft.

say again: Used to request a repeat of the last transmission. Usually specifies transmission or the portion not understood, e.g., "Say again all after Abram VOR."

say altitude: Used by ATC to ascertain an aircraft's specific altitude or flight level. When climbing or descending, the pilot should state his indicated altitude rounded-off to the nearest 100 feet.

say heading: Used by ATC to request an aircraft's heading. The pilot should state the actual heading of the aircraft.

sea lane: A designated portion of water outlined by visual surface markers for and intended to be used by seaplanes.

Search and Rescue (SAR): A service that seeks missing aircraft and assists those in trouble. It is a cooperative effort; the US Coast Guard coordinates SAR for the maritime region, the USAF, the inland region. Information pertinent to SAR should be passed through any ATC facility.

see and avoid: A visual procedure wherein pilots of aircraft flying in visual meteorological conditions (VMC), regardless of type of flight plan, are charged with the responsibility to observe the presence of other aircraft and to maneuver as required to avoid the other aircraft.

segmented circle: A system of visual indicators designed to provide traffic pattern information at airports without operating control towers.

separation minima: The minimum longitudinal, lateral, or vertical distances by which aircraft are spaced through the application of ATC procedures.

short range clearance: A clearance issued to a departing IFR flight which authorizes IFR flight to a specific fix short of the destination while ATC gets its act together.

sidestep maneuver: A visual maneuver accomplished by a pilot at the completion of an instrument approach to permit a straight-in landing on a parallel runway not more than 1,200 feet to either side of the runway to which the instrument approach was conducted.

SIGMET (Significant Meteorological Information): A weather advisory significant to the safety of all aircraft; it covers severe and extreme turbulence, severe icing, and widespread dust or sandstorms that reduce visibility to less than three miles.

Simplified Directional Facility (SDF): A navaid used for nonprecision instrument approaches. The final approach course is similar to that of an ILS localizer except that the SDF course may be offset from the runway, generally not more than three degrees, and the course may be wider than the localizer, resulting in a lesser degree of accuracy.

simultaneous ILS/MLS approaches: An approach system permitting simultaneous ILS/MLS approaches to airports having parallel runways separated by at least 4,300 feet between centerlines.

single direction routes: Preferred IFR Routes that are sometimes depicted on high altitude en route charts and which are normally flown in one direction only.

special emergency: A condition of air piracy or other hostile act by a person(s) aboard an aircraft which threatens the safety of the aircraft or its passengers.

Special Use Airspace: Airspace of defined dimensions identified by an area on the surface of the earth wherein activities must be confined because of their nature and/or wherein limitations may be imposed upon aircraft operations that are not part of those activities. The types of Special Use Airspace are:

- Alert Area—A high volume of pilot training or an unusual type of aerial activity—Refer to *AIM*.

- Controlled Firing Area.

- Military Operations Area (MOA).

- Prohibited Area—Refer to air charts and *AIM*.

- Restricted Area—Designated under FAR Part 73.

- Warning Area—Refers to international airspace.

Special VFR Operations: Aircraft operating in accordance with clearance within control zones in weather conditions less than the basic VFR minima. Such operations must be requested by the pilot and approved by ATC.

squawk (mode, code, function): Activate specific modes or codes or functions on the aircraft transponder.

Standard Instrument Departure (SID): A preplanned instrument flight rule (IFR) ATC departure procedure printed for pilot use in graphic and/or textual form. SIDs provide transition from the terminal to the appropriate en route structure.

standard rate turn: A turn of three degrees per second.

Standard Terminal Arrival (STAR): A preplanned Instrument Flight Rule ATC arrival procedure published in graphic and/or textual form. STARs provide transition from the en route structure to an outer fix or an instrument approach fix/arrival waypoint in the terminal area.

stand by: Means the pilot or controller must pause for a few seconds, usually to attend to other duties of higher priority. It also means to wait, as in "Stand by for clearance."

stepdown fix: A fix permitting additional descent within a segment of an instrument approach procedure by identifying a point at which a controlling obstacle has been safety overflown.

step turn: A maneuver used to put a floatplane in a planing configuration prior to entering an active sea lane for takeoff.

stereo route: A routinely used route of flight established by users and ARTCCs identified by a coded name, e.g., ALPHA 2.

stopover flight plan: A flight plan format that permits in a single submission the filing of a sequence of flight plans through interim full-stop destinations to a final destination.

stop squawk (mode or code): Used by ATC to tell a pilot to turn off specified functions of the aircraft's transponder.

stopway: An area beyond the takeoff runway designated by the airport authorities as able to support an airplane during an aborted takeoff.

straight-in approach (IFR): An instrument approach wherein final approach is begun without first having executed a procedure turn, not necessarily completed with a straight-in landing or made to straight-in landing minimums.

straight-in approach (VFR): Entry into the traffic pattern by interception of the extended runway centerline (final approach course) without executing any other portion of the traffic pattern.

straight-in landing: A landing made on a runway aligned within 30 degrees of the final approach course (following completion of an instrument approach).

sunrise and **sunset:** The mean solar times of sunrise and sunset as published in the *Nautical Almanac,* converted to local standard time.

super high frequency (SHF): The frequency band between 3 and 30 gigahertz (GHz). The elevation and azimuth stations of the microwave landing system operate from 5031 to 5091 MHz in this spectrum.

Surveillance Approach: An instrument approach wherein the controller issues instructions, for pilot compliance, based on aircraft position in relation to the final approach course (azimuth), and the distance (range) from the end of the runway as displayed on the controller's radar scope. See *PAR Approach.*

taxi into position and hold: Used by ATC to inform a pilot to taxi onto the departure runway in takeoff position and hold. It is *not* authorization for takeoff.

terminal area: A general term used to describe airspace in which approach control service or airport traffic control service is provided.

Terminal Control Area: See *Controlled Airspace;* TCA in *AIM.*

Terminal Radar Program: A national program instituted to extend the terminal radar service provided IFR aircraft to VFR aircraft. Pilot participation in the program is urged by FAA/ATC but is not mandatory. The program is divided into two parts and referred to as "Stage II" and "Stage III." The stage service provided at a particular location is listed in the Airport/Facility Directory.

Stage I originally comprised basic radar services [but the term is no longer in use].

Stage II, Radar Advisory and Sequencing for VFR Aircraft—Provides, in addition to the basic radar services, vectoring and sequencing on a full-time basis to arriving VFR aircraft. The purpose is to adjust the flow of arriving IFR and VFR aircraft into the traffic pattern, and to provide traffic advisories to departing VFR aircraft.

Stage III, Radar Sequencing and Separation Service for VFR Aircraft—Provides, in addition to the basic radar services and Stage II, separation between all participating VFR aircraft. The purpose is to provide separation between all participating VFR aircraft and all IFR aircraft operating within the airspace defined as a Terminal Radar Service Area (TRSA) or Terminal Control Area (TCA).

Terminal Radar Service Area (TRSA): Airspace surrounding designated airports wherein ATC provides radar vectoring, sequencing, and separation on a full-time basis for all IFR and for participating VFR aircraft. The service provided in a TRSA is Stage III. TRSAs are shown on VFR aeronautical charts. Pilot participation is urged but not mandatory.

tetrahedron: A device normally located on uncontrolled airports and used as a landing direction indicator. The small end of a tetrahedron points in the direction of landing. At controlled airports . . . the tetrahedron should be disregarded . . .

that is correct: "The understanding you have is right."

threshold: The beginning of that portion of the runway usable for landing.

Threshold Crossing Height (TCH): The theoretical height above the runway threshold at which the aircraft's glideslope antenna would be if the aircraft maintains the trajectory established by the mean ILS glideslope or MLS glide path.

torching: The burning of fuel at the end of an exhaust pipe of a reciprocating engine, the result of an excessively rich fuel to air mixture.

touchdown zone: The first 3,000 feet of the runway, beginning at the threshold.

Touchdown Zone Elevation (TDZE): The highest elevation in the first 3,000 feet of the runway or landing surface. TDZE is indicated on the instrument approach procedure chart when straight-in landing minimums are authorized.

Tower (Airport Traffic Control Tower): A terminal facility that uses air-ground communications, visual signaling, and other devices to provide ATC services to aircraft operating in the vicinity of an airport or on the movement area.

Tower En Route Control Service (Tower-to-Tower): The control of IFR en route traffic within delegated airspace between two or more adjacent approach control facilities. This service is designed to expedite traffic and reduce control and pilot communications requirements.

track: The actual flight path of an aircraft over the surface of the earth

Traffic Advisories: Advisories used to alert pilots to other known or observed traffic that may be in such proximity to warrant attention. The word "Traffic" followed by additional information is used, e.g., "Traffic, two o'clock, one-zero miles, southbound, eight thousand." Never assume that ATC is aware of all traffic in the area. "See and avoid" is every pilot's responsibility.

traffic in sight: Used by pilots to inform a controller that previously issued traffic is in sight. [The opposite is "negative contact," or as the Top Guns, "No joy."]

traffic pattern: The traffic flow that is prescribed for aircraft landing at, taxiing on, or taking off from an airport. The components of a typical traffic pattern are upwind leg, crosswind leg, downwind leg, base leg, and final approach:

- *Upwind leg*—A flight path parallel to the landing runway in the direction of landing.

- *Crosswind leg*—A flight path at right angles to the landing runway off its upwind end.

- *Downwind leg*—A flight path parallel to the landing runway in the direction opposite to landing. It normally extends between the crosswind leg and the base leg.

- *Base leg*—A flight path at right angles to the landing runway off its approach end. The base leg normally extends from the downwind leg to the intersection of the extended runway centerline.

- *Final approach*—A flight path in the direction of landing along the extended runway centerline. The final approach normally extends from base leg to the runway.

Transcribed Weather Broadcast (TWEB): A continuous recording of meteorological and aeronautical information that is broadcast on L/MF and VOR facilities for pilots.

transmissometer: An apparatus used to determine visibility by measuring the transmission of light through the atmosphere. It is employed to determine runway visual range (RVR).

transmitting in the blind: Transmitting from one station to other stations where two-way communication cannot be established, but where it is believed that the called stations may be able to receive the transmission.

transponder: The airborne radar beacon receiver/transmitter portion of the Air Traffic Control Radar Beacon System (ATCRBS) which automatically receives radio signals from interrogators on the ground, and selectively replies with a specific pulse or pulse group.

T-VOR (Terminal VOR): A VOR station located on or near an airport and used as an approach aid.

unable: Indicates inability to comply with a specific ATC instruction, request, or clearance.

Uncontrolled Airspace: That portion of the airspace that not designated as Continental Control Area, a Control Area, Control Zone,

Terminal Control Area, or Transition Area and within which ATC has neither the authority nor the responsibility for exercising control over air traffic.

UNICOM: A nongovernment communication facility that may provide airport information at certain airports. Locations and frequencies are shown on aeronautical charts and Airport/Facility Directory.

vector: A heading issued to an aircraft to provide navigational guidance by radar.

verify: Request confirmation of information, e.g., "Verify assigned altitude."

very high frequency (VHF): The frequency band between 30 and 300 MHz. Portions of this band, 108 to 118 MHz, are used for certain navaids; 118 to 136 MHz are used for civil air/ground voice communications.

very low frequency (VLF): The frequency band between 3 and 30 kHz.

VFR aircraft: An aircraft operated in accordance with Visual Flight Rules.

VFR conditions: Weather conditions equal to or better than the minimum for flight under Visual Flight Rules. The term may be used as an ATC clearance/instruction only when:

- An IFR aircraft requests a climb or descent in VFR conditions.

- The clearance will result in noise abatement benefits where part of the IFR departure route does not conform to an FAA-approved noise abatement route or altitude.

- A pilot has requested a practice instrument approach and is not on an IFR flight plan.

All pilots receiving this authorization must comply with the VFR visibility and distance-from-cloud criteria in FAR Part 91.

VFR on top: ATC authorization for an IFR aircraft to operate in VFR conditions at any appropriate VFR altitude (as specified in FAR and as is restricted by ATC). See Part 91.

visibility: The ability, as determined by atmospheric conditions and expressed in units of distance, to see and identify prominent unlighted objects by day and prominent lighted objects by night. Visibility is reported as statute miles, hundreds of feet, or meters.

Flight visibility—The average forward horizontal distance, from the cockpit of an aircraft in flight, at which prominent unlighted objects may be seen and identified by day and prominent lighted objects may be seen and identified by night.

Ground visibility—The prevailing horizontal visibility near the earth's surface as reported by the U.S. National Weather Service or an accredited observer.

Prevailing visibility—The greatest horizontal visibility equaled or exceeded throughout at least half the horizon circle which need not necessarily be continuous.

Runway Visibility Value (RVV)—The visibility determined for a particular runway by a transmissometer. RVV is used in lieu of prevailing visibility in determining minimums for a particular runway.

Runway Visual Range (RVR)—An instrumentally derived value, based on standard calibrations, that represents the horizontal distance a pilot will see down the runway from the approach end. RVR, in contrast to prevailing or runway visibility, is based on what a pilot in a moving aircraft should see looking down the runway.

- *Touchdown RVR*—The RVR visibility readout values obtained from RVR equipment serving the touch-down zone.

- *Mid RVR*—The RVR readout values obtained from RVR equipment located midfield of the runway.

- *Rollout RVR*—The RVR readout values obtained from RVR equipment located nearest the rollout end of the runway.

Visual Approach: An approach wherein an aircraft on an IFR flight plan, operating in VFR conditions under the control of an ATC facility and having an ATC authorization, may proceed to the airport of destination in VFR conditions.

Visual Descent Point (VDP): A defined point on the final approach course of a nonprecision straight-in approach procedure from which normal descent from the MDA to the runway touchdown point may be started, provided the approach threshold of that runway, or approach lights, or other markings identifiable with the approach end of the runway are clearly visible to the pilot.

Visual Flight Rules (VFR): Rules that govern the procedures for conducting flight under visual conditions. The term "VFR" is also used in the U.S. to indicate weather conditions that are equal to or greater than minimum VFR requirements. It is also used to indicate the type of flight plan.

visual holding: The holding of aircraft at selected, prominent geographical fixes that can be easily recognized from the air.

VORTAC: A co-located VOR and TACAN, the TACAN providing DME.

VOR (Very High Frequency Omnidirectional Range Station): A ground-based electronic navigation aid transmitting VHF signals, 360 degrees in azimuth, oriented from magnetic north. The VOR periodically identifies itself by Morse Code and may have an additional voice identification feature. Voice features may be used by ATC or FSS for transmitting instructions/information to pilots.

wake turbulence: Phenomena resulting from the passage of an aircraft through the atmosphere. The term includes vortices, thrust stream turbulence, jet blast, jet wash, propeller wash, and rotor wash, both on the ground and in the air.

waypoint: A predetermined geographical position used for route and/or instrument approach definition, or progress reporting purposes, that is defined relative to a VORTAC station or in terms of longitude/latitude coordinates.

Weather Advisory (WS, WST, WA, CWA): In aviation weather forecast practice, an expression of hazardous weather conditions not predicted in the area forecast, as they affect the operation of air traffic and as prepared by the NWS.

when able: When used in conjunction with ATC instructions, gives the pilot the latitude to delay compliance until a condition or event has been reconciled. Unlike "pilot discretion," when instructions are prefaced "when able," the pilot is expected to seek the first opportunity to comply.

wilco: "I have received your message, understand it, and will comply with it" [seldom heard anymore].

wind shear: A change in wind velocity and/or direction in a short distance, resulting in a tearing or shearing effect. It can exist in a horizontal or vertical direction or both.

words twice:

- As a request: "Communication is difficult; please say every phrase twice."

- As information: "Because communications are difficult, every phase in this message will be spoken twice."

Appendix D

Private Pilot
Airplane
Single-Engine Land
Practical Test Standard

I. AREA OF OPERATION:
PREFLIGHT PREPARATION

A. TASK: CERTIFICATES AND DOCUMENTS (ASEL)

PILOT OPERATION – 1

REFERENCES: FAR Parts 61 and 91; AC 61-21,
AC 61-23; Pilot's Handbook and Flight Manual.

Objective. To determine that the applicant:

1. Exhibits knowledge by explaining the appropriate –

   (a) pilot certificate, privileges and limitations.
   (b) medical certificate, class and duration.
   (c) personal pilot logbook or flight record.
   (d) FCC station license and operator's permit, as required.

2. Exhibits knowledge by locating and explaining the significance and importance of the –

   (a) airworthiness and registration certificates.
   (b) operating limitations, handbooks, or manuals.
   (c) equipment list.
   (d) weight and balance data.
   (e) maintenance requirements and appropriate records.

B. TASK: OBTAINING WEATHER INFORMATION (ASEL)

NOTE: This TASK is NOT required for the addition of a single–engine land class rating.

PILOT OPERATION – 1

REFERENCES: AC 00-6, AC 00-45, AC 61-21,
AC 61-23, AC 61-84.

Objective. To determine that the applicant:

1. Exhibits knowledge of aviation weather information by obtaining, reading, and analyzing –

   (a) weather reports and forecasts.
   (b) weather charts.
   (c) pilot weather reports.
   (d) SIGMET's and AIRMET's.
   (e) Notices to Airmen.
   (f) wind–shear reports.

2. Makes a competent go/no–go decision based on the available weather information.

C. TASK: DETERMINING PERFORMANCE AND LIMITATIONS (ASEL)

PILOT OPERATION – 1

REFERENCES: AC 61-21, AC 61-23, AC 61-84;
Airplane Handbook and Flight Manual.

Objective. To determine that the applicant:

1. Exhibits knowledge by explaining airplane weight and balance, performance, and limitations, including adverse aerodynamic effects of exceeding the limits.
2. Uses available and appropriate performance charts, tables, and data.
3. Computes weight and balance, and determines that weight and center of gravity will be within limits during all phases of the flight.
4. Calculates airplane performance, considering density altitude, wind, terrain, and other pertinent conditions.
5. Describes the effects of atmospheric conditions on airplane performance.

6. Makes a competent decision on whether the required performance is within the operating limitations of the airplane.

D. TASK: CROSS–COUNTRY FLIGHT PLANNING (ASEL)

NOTE: This TASK is NOT required for the addition of a single–engine land class rating.

PILOT OPERATION – 7

REFERENCES: AC 61-21, AC 61-23, AC 61-84.

Objective. To determine that the applicant:

1. Exhibits knowledge by planning, within 30 minutes, a VFR cross–country flight of a duration near the range of the airplane, considering fuel and loading.
2. Selects and uses current and appropriate aeronautical charts.
3. Plots a course for the intended route of flight with fuel stops, if necessary.
4. Selects prominent en route check points.
5. Computes the flight time, headings, and fuel requirements.
6. Selects appropriate radio navigation aids and communication facilities.
7. Identifies airspace, obstructions, and alternate airports.
8. Extracts pertinent information from the Airport/Facility Directory and other flight publications, including NOTAM's.
9. Completes a navigation log.
10. Completes and files a VFR flight plan.

E. TASK: AIRPLANE SYSTEMS (ASEL)

PILOT OPERATION – 1

REFERENCES: AC 61-21; Airplane Handbook and Flight Manual.

Objective. To determine that the applicant exhibits knowledge by explaining the airplane systems and operation including, as appropriate:

1. Primary flight controls and trim.
2. Wing flaps, leading edge devices, and spoilers.
3. Flight instruments.
4. Landing gear.
5. Engine.
6. Propeller.
7. Fuel system.
8. Hydraulic system.
9. Electrical system.
10. Environmental system.
11. Oil system.
12. Deice and anti–ice systems.
13. Avionics.
14. Vacuum system.

F. TASK: AEROMEDICAL FACTORS (ASEL)

PILOT OPERATION – 1

REFERENCES: AC 61-21, AC 67-2; AIM.

Objective. To determine that the applicant:

1. Exhibits knowledge of the elements related to aeromedical factors, including the symptoms, effects, and corrective action of –

   (a) hypoxia.
   (b) hyperventilation.

   (c) middle ear and sinus problems.
   (d) spatial disorientation.
   (e) motion sickness.
   (f) carbon monoxide poisoning.

2. Exhibits knowledge of the effects of alcohol and drugs, and the relationship to flight safety.
3. Exhibits knowledge of nitrogen excesses during scuba dives, and how this affects a pilot or passenger during flight.

II. AREA OF OPERATION:
GROUND OPERATIONS

A. TASK: VISUAL INSPECTION (ASEL)

PILOT OPERATION – 1

REFERENCES: AC 61-21; Airplane Handbook and Flight Manual.

Objective. To determine that the applicant:

1. Exhibits knowledge of airplane visual inspection by explaining the reasons for checking all items.
2. Inspects the airplane by following a checklist.
3. Determines that the airplane is in condition for safe flight emphasizing –

   (a) fuel quantity, grade, and type.
   (b) fuel contamination safeguards.
   (c) fuel venting.
   (d) oil quantity, grade, and type.
   (e) fuel, oil, and hydraulic leaks.
   (f) flight controls.
   (g) structural damage.
   (h) exhaust system.
   (i) tiedown, control lock, and wheel chock removal.
   (j) ice and frost removal.
   (k) security of baggage, cargo, and, equipment.

B. TASK: COCKPIT MANAGEMENT (ASEL)

PILOT OPERATION – 1

REFERENCE: AC 61-21.

Objective. To determine that the applicant:

1. Exhibits knowledge of cockpit management by explaining related safety and efficiency factors.
2. Organizes and arranges the material and equipment in an efficient manner.
3. Ensures that the safety belts and shoulder harnesses are fastened.
4. Adjusts and locks the rudder pedals and pilot's seat to a safe position and ensures full control movement.
5. Briefs occupants on the use of safety belts and emergency procedures.
6. Exhibits adequate crew coordination.

C. TASK: STARTING ENGINE (ASEL)

PILOT OPERATION – 1

REFERENCES: AC 61-21, AC 61-23, AC 91-13, AC 91-55; Airplane Handbook and Flight Manual.

Objective. To determine that the applicant:

1. Exhibits knowledge by explaining engine starting procedures, including starting under various atmospheric conditions.

2. Performs all the items on the checklist.
3. Accomplishes correct starting procedures with emphasis on –

   (a) positioning the airplane to avoid creating hazards.
   (b) determining that the area is clear.
   (c) adjusting the engine controls.
   (d) setting the brakes.
   (e) preventing airplane movement after engine start.
   (f) avoiding excessive engine RPM and temperatures.
   (g) checking the engine instruments after engine start.

D. TASK: TAXIING (ASEL)

PILOT OPERATION – 2

REFERENCE: AC 61-21.

Objective.   To determine that the applicant:

1. Exhibits knowledge by explaining safe taxi procedures.
2. Adheres to signals and clearances, and follows the proper taxi route.
3. Performs a brake check immediately after the airplane begins moving.
4. Controls taxi speed without excessive use of brakes.
5. Recognizes and avoids hazards.
6. Positions the controls for the existing wind conditions.
7. Avoids careless and reckless operations.

E. TASK: PRETAKEOFF CHECK (ASEL)

PILOT OPERATION – 1

REFERENCES: AC 61-21; Airplane Handbook and Flight Manual.

Objective.   To determine that the applicant:

1. Exhibits knowledge of the pretakeoff check by explaining the reasons for checking all items.
2. Positions the airplane to avoid creating hazards.
3. Divides attention inside and outside of the cockpit.
4. Accomplishes the checklist items.
5. Ensures that the airplane is in safe operating condition.
6. Reviews the critical takeoff performance airspeeds and distances.
7. Describes takeoff emergency procedures.
8. Obtains and interprets takeoff and departure clearances.

F. TASK: POSTFLIGHT PROCEDURES (ASEL)

PILOT OPERATION – 3

REFERENCES: AC 61-21; Airplane Handbook and Flight Manual.

Objective.   To determine that the applicant:

1. Exhibits knowledge by explaining the postflight procedures, including taxiing, parking, shutdown, securing, and postflight inspection.
2. Selects and taxies to the designated or suitable parking area, considering wind conditions and obstructions.
3. Parks the airplane properly.
4. Follows the recommended procedure for engine shutdown, cockpit securing, and deplaning passengers.
5. Secures the airplane properly.
6. Performs a satisfactory postflight inspection.

III. AREA OF OPERATION:
AIRPORT AND TRAFFIC PATTERN OPERATIONS

NOTE: This AREA OF OPERATION is NOT required for the addition of a single–engine land class rating.

A. TASK: RADIO COMMUNICATIONS AND ATC LIGHT SIGNALS (ASEL)

PILOT OPERATION – 2

REFERENCES: AC 61-21, AC 61-23; AIM.

Objective.   To determine that the applicant:

1. Exhibits knowledge by explaining radio communication, ATC light signals, procedures at controlled and uncontrolled airports, and prescribed procedures for radio failure.
2. Selects the appropriate frequencies for the facilities to be used.
3. Transmits requests and reports using the recommended standard phraseology.
4. Receives, acknowledges, and complies with radio communications.

B. TASK: TRAFFIC PATTERN OPERATIONS (ASEL)

PILOT OPERATION – 2

REFERENCES: AC 61-21, AC 61-23; AIM.

Objective.   To determine that the applicant:

1. Exhibits knowledge by explaining traffic pattern procedures at controlled and uncontrolled airports, including collision, wind shear, and wake turbulence avoidance.
2. Follows the established traffic pattern procedures according to instructions or rules.
3. Corrects for wind drift to follow the appropriate ground track.
4. Maintains proper spacing from other traffic.
5. Maintains the traffic pattern altitude, ±100 feet.
6. Maintains the desired airspeed, ±10 knots.
7. Completes the prelanding cockpit checklist.
8. Maintains orientation with the runway in use.

C. TASK: AIRPORT AND RUNWAY MARKING AND LIGHTING (ASEL)

PILOT OPERATION – 2

REFERENCES: AC 61-21; AIM.

Objective.   To determine that the applicant:

1. Exhibits knowledge by explaining airport and runway markings and lighting aids.
2. Identifies and interprets airport, runway, taxiway marking, and lighting aids.

IV. AREA OF OPERATION:
TAKEOFFS AND CLIMBS

A. TASK: NORMAL AND CROSSWIND TAKEOFFS AND CLIMBS (ASEL)

PILOT OPERATION – 5

REFERENCES: AC 61-21; Airplane Handbook and Flight Manual.

Objective.   To determine that the applicant:

1. Exhibits knowledge by explaining the elements of normal and crosswind takeoffs and climbs, including airspeeds, configurations, and emergency procedures.

2. Selects the recommended wing–flap setting.
3. Aligns the airplane on the runway centerline.
4. Applies aileron deflection properly.
5. Advances the throttle smoothly to maximum allowable power.
6. Checks engine instruments.
7. Maintains directional control on runway centerline.
8. Adjusts aileron deflection during acceleration.
9. Rotates at the recommended[1] airspeed and accelerates to V_Y and establishes wind–drift correction.
10. Establishes the pitch attitude for V_Y and maintains V_Y, ±5 knots.
11. Retracts the wing flaps, as recommended, or at a safe altitude.
12. Retracts the landing gear, if retractable, after a positive rate of climb has been established and a safe landing can no longer be accomplished on the remaining runway.
13. Maintains takeoff power to a safe maneuvering altitude.
14. Maintains a straight track over the extended runway centerline until a turn is required.
15. Completes after–takeoff checklist.

NOTE: If a crosswind condition does not exist, the applicant's knowledge of the TASK will be evaluated through oral testing.

B. TASK: SHORT–FIELD TAKEOFF AND CLIMB (ASEL)

PILOT OPERATION – 8

REFERENCES: AC 61-21; Airplane Handbook and Flight Manual.

Objective. To determine that the applicant:

1. Exhibits knowledge by explaining the elements of a short–field takeoff and climb, including the significance of appropriate airspeeds and configurations, emergency procedures, and expected performance for existing operating conditions.
2. Selects the recommended wing–flap setting.
3. Positions the airplane at the beginning of the takeoff runway aligned on the runway centerline.
4. Advances the throttle smoothly to maximum allowable power.
5. Maintains directional control on the runway centerline.
6. Rotates at the recommended airspeed and accelerates to V_X.
7. Climbs at V_X or recommended airspeed, +5, –0 knots until obstacle is cleared, or until at least 50 feet above the surface, then accelerates to V_Y and maintains V_Y ±5 knots.
8. Retracts the wing flaps, as recommended, or at a safe altitude.
9. Retracts the landing gear, if retractable, after a positive rate of climb has been established and a safe landing can no longer be accomplished on the remaining runway.
10. Maintains takeoff power to a safe maneuvering altitude.
11. Maintains a straight track over the extended runway centerline until a turn is required.
12. Completes after–takeoff checklist.

C. TASK: SOFT–FIELD TAKEOFF AND CLIMB (ASEL)

PILOT OPERATION – 8

REFERENCES: AC 61-21; Airplane Handbook and Flight Manual.

[1]The term ''recommended'' refers to the manufacturer's recommendation. If the manufacturer's recommendation is not available, the description in AC 61–21 will be used.

Objective. To determine that the applicant:

1. Exhibits knowledge by explaining the elements of a soft–field takeoff and climb, including the significance of appropriate airspeeds and configurations, emergency procedures, and hazards associated with climbing at an airspeed less than V_X.
2. Selects the recommended wing–flap setting.
3. Taxies onto the takeoff surface at a speed consistent with safety.
4. Aligns the airplane on takeoff path, without stopping, and advances the throttle smoothly to maximum allowable power.
5. Adjusts and maintains a pitch attitude which transfers the weight from the wheels to the wings as rapidly as possible.
6. Maintains directional control on the center of the takeoff path.
7. Lifts off at the lowest possible airspeed and remains in ground effect while accelerating.
8. Accelerates to and maintains V_X +5, –0 knots, if obstructions must be cleared, otherwise to V_Y ±5 knots.
9. Retracts the wing flaps, as recommended, and at a safe altitude.
10. Retracts the landing gear, if retractable, after a positive rate of climb has been establsihed and a landing can no longer be accomplished on the remaining runway.
11. Maintains takeoff power to a safe maneuvering altitude.
12. Maintains a straight track over the center of the extended takeoff path until a turn is required.
13. Completes after–takeoff checklist.

V. AREA OF OPERATION:
CROSS–COUNTRY FLYING

NOTE: This AREA OF OPERATION is NOT required for the addition of a single–engine land class rating.

A. TASK: PILOTAGE AND DEAD RECKONING (ASEL)

PILOT OPERATION – 7

REFERENCES: AC 61-21, AC 61-23.

Objective. To determine that the applicant:

1. Exhibits knowledge by explaining pilotage and dead reckoning techniques and procedures.
2. Follows the preplanned course solely by visual reference to landmarks.
3. Identifies landmarks by relating the surface features to chart symbols.
4. Navigates by means of precomputed headings, groundspeed, and elapsed time.
5. Combines pilotage and dead reckoning.
6. Verifies the airplane position within 3 nautical miles of the flight planned route at all times.
7. Arrives at the en route checkpoints and destination ±5 minutes of the initial or revised ETA.
8. Corrects for, and records, the differences between preflight fuel, groundspeed, and heading calculations and those determined en route.
9. Maintains the selected altitudes, within ±200 feet.
10. Maintains the desired heading, ±10°.
11. Follows the climb, cruise, and descent checklists.

B. TASK: RADIO NAVIGATION (ASEL)

PILOT OPERATION – 7

REFERENCES: AC 61-21, AC 61-23.

Objective.   To determine that the applicant:

1. Exhibits knowledge by explaining radio navigation, equipment, procedures, and limitations.
2. Selects and identifies the desired radio facility.
3. Locates position relative to the radio navigation facility.
4. Intercepts and tracks a given radial or bearing.
5. Locates position using cross radials or bearings.
6. Recognizes or describes the indication of station passage.
7. Recognizes signal loss and takes appropriate action.
8. Maintains the appropriate altitude, ±200 feet.

C.   TASK: DIVERSION (ASEL)

PILOT OPERATION − 7

REFERENCES: AC 61-21, AC 61-23.

Objective.   To determine that the applicant:

1. Exhibits knowledge by explaining the procedures for diverting, including the recognition of adverse weather conditions.
2. Selects an appropriate alternate airport and route.
3. Diverts toward the alternate airport promptly.
4. Makes a reasonable estimate of heading, groundspeed, arrival time, and fuel consumption to the alternate airport.
5. Maintains the appropriate altitude, ±200 feet.

D.   TASK: LOST PROCEDURES (ASEL)

PILOT OPERATION − 7

REFERENCES: AC 61-21, AC 61-23.

Objective.   To determine that the applicant:

1. Exhibits knowledge by explaining lost procedures, including the reasons for −

   (a) maintaining the original or an appropriate heading, identifying landmarks, and climbing, if necessary.
   (b) proceeding to and identifying the nearest concentration of prominent landmarks.
   (c) using available radio navigation aids or contacting an appropriate facility for assistance.
   (d) planning a precautionary landing if deteriorating visibility and/or fuel exhaustion is imminent.

2. Selects the best course of action when given a lost situation.

VI.   AREA OF OPERATION:
FLIGHT BY REFERENCE TO INSTRUMENTS

NOTE: This AREA OF OPERATION is NOT required for the addition of a single−engine land class rating.

A.   TASK: STRAIGHT−AND−LEVEL FLIGHT (ASEL)

PILOT OPERATION − 6

REFERENCES: AC 61-21, AC 61-23, AC 61-27.

Objective.   To determine that the applicant:

1. Exhibits knowledge by explaining flight solely by reference to instruments as related to straight−and−level flight.
2. Makes smooth and coordinated control applications.

3. Maintains straight−and−level flight for at least 3 minutes.
4. Maintains the desired heading, ±10°.
5. Maintains the desired altitude, ±100 feet.
6. Maintains the desired airspeed, ±10 knots.

B.   TASK: STRAIGHT, CONSTANT AIRSPEED CLIMBS (ASEL)

PILOT OPERATION − 6

REFERENCES: AC 61-21, AC 61-23, AC 61-27.

Objective.   To determine that the applicant:

1. Exhibits knowledge by explaining flight solely by reference to instruments as related to straight, constant airspeed climbs.
2. Establishes the climb pitch attitude and power setting on an assigned heading.
3. Makes smooth and coordinated control applications.
4. Maintains the desired heading, ±10°.
5. Maintains the desired airspeed, ±10 knots.
6. Levels off at the desired altitude, ±100 feet.

C.   TASK: STRAIGHT, CONSTANT AIRSPEED DESCENTS (ASEL)

PILOT OPERATION − 6

REFERENCES: AC 61-21, AC 61-23, AC 61-27.

Objective.   To determine that the applicant:

1. Exhibits knowledge by explaining flight solely by reference to instruments as related to straight, constant airspeed descents.
2. Determines the minimum safe altitude at which the descent should be terminated.
3. Establishes the descent configuration, pitch, and power setting on the assigned heading.
4. Makes smooth and coordinated control applications.
5. Maintains the desired heading, ±10°.
6. Maintains the desired airspeed, ±10 knots.
7. Levels off at the desired altitude, ±100 feet.

D.   TASK: TURNS TO HEADINGS (ASEL)

PILOT OPERATION − 6

REFERENCES: AC 61-21, AC 61-23, AC 61-27.

Objective.   To determine that the applicant:

1. Exhibits knowledge by explaining flight solely by reference to instruments as related to turns to headings.
2. Enters and maintains approximately a standard−rate turn with smooth and coordinated control applications.
3. Maintains the desired altitude, ±100 feet.
4. Maintains the desired airspeed, ±10 knots.
5. Maintains the desired bank angle.
6. Rolls out at the desired heading, ±10°.

E.   TASK: UNUSUAL FLIGHT ATTITUDES (ASEL)

PILOT OPERATION − 6

REFERENCES: AC 61-21, AC 61-23, AC 61-27.

NOTE: Unusual flight attitudes, such as a start of a power−on spiral or an approach to a climbing stall, shall not exceed 45° bank or 10° pitch from level flight.

Objective.   To determine that the applicant:

1. Exhibits knowledge by explaining flight solely by reference to instruments as related to unusual flight attitudes.
2. Recognizes unusual flight attitudes promptly.
3. Properly interprets the instruments.
4. Recovers to a stabilized level flight attitude by prompt, smooth, coordinated control, applied in the proper sequence.
5. Avoids excessive load factor, airspeed, and stall.

F. **TASK:** **RADIO AIDS AND RADAR SERVICES** (ASEL)

PILOT OPERATION – 6

REFERENCES: AC 61-21, AC 61-23, AC 61-27.

Objective. To determine that the applicant:

1. Exhibits knowledge by explaining radio aids and radar services available for use during flight solely by reference to instruments.
2. Selects, tunes, and identifies the appropriate facility.
3. Follows verbal instructions or radio navigation aids for guidance.
4. Determines the minimum safe altitude.
5. Maintains the desired altitude, ±100 feet.
6. Maintains the desired heading, ±10°.

VII. AREA OF OPERATION:
FLIGHT AT CRITICALLY SLOW AIRSPEEDS

A. **TASK:** **FULL STALLS — POWER OFF** (ASEL)

PILOT OPERATION – 4

REFERENCE: AC 61-21.

Objective. To determine that the applicant:

1. Exhibits knowledge by explaining the aerodynamic factors and flight situations that may result in full stalls — power off, including proper recovery procedures, and hazards of stalling during uncoordinated flight.
2. Selects an entry altitude that will allow the recoveries to be completed no lower than 1,500 feet AGL.
3. Establishes the normal approach or landing configuration and airspeed with the throttle closed or at a reduced power setting.
4. Establishes a straight glide or a gliding turn with a bank angle of 30°, ±10°, in coordinated flight.
5. Establishes and maintains a landing pitch attitude that will induce a full stall.
6. Recognizes the indications of a full stall and promptly recovers by decreasing the angle of attack, leveling the wings, and adjusting the power, as necessary, to regain normal flight attitude.
7. Retracts the wing flaps and landing gear (if retractable) and establishes straight–and–level flight or climb.
8. Avoids secondary stalls, excessive airspeed, excessive altitude loss, spins, and flight below 1,500 feet AGL.

B. **TASK:** **FULL STALLS — POWER ON** (ASEL)

PILOT OPERATION – 4

REFERENCE: AC 61-21.

Objective. To determine that the applicant:

1. Exhibits knowledge by explaining the aerodynamic factors and flight situations that may result in full

stalls — power on, including proper recovery procedures, and hazards of stalling during uncoordinated flight.
2. Selects an entry altitude that will allow recoveries to be completed no lower than 1,500 feet AGL.
3. Establishes takeoff or normal climb configuration.
4. Establishes takeoff or climb airspeed before applying takeoff or climb power. (Reduced power may be used to avoid excessive pitch–up during entry only.)
5. Establishes and maintains a pitch attitude straight ahead or in a turn with a bank angle of 20°, ±10°, that will induce a full stall.
6. Applies proper control to maintain coordinated flight.
7. Recognizes the indications of a full stall and promptly recovers by decreasing the angle of attack, leveling the wings, and adjusting the power, as necessary, to regain normal flight attitude.
8. Retracts the wing flaps and landing gear (if retractable) and establishes straight–and–level flight or climb.
9. Avoids secondary stall, excessive airspeed, excessive altitude loss, spin, and flight below 1,500 feet AGL.

C. **TASK:** **IMMINENT STALLS — POWER ON AND POWER OFF** (ASEL)

PILOT OPERATION – 4

REFERENCE: AC 61-21.

Objective. To determine that the applicant:

1. Exhibits knowledge by explaining the aerodynamic factors associated with imminent stalls (power on and power off), an awareness of speed loss in different configurations, and the procedure for resuming normal flight attitude.
2. Selects an entry altitude that will allow recoveries to be completed no lower than 1,500 feet AGL.
3. Establishes either a takeoff, a climb, or an approach configuration with the appropriate power setting.
4. Establishes a pitch attitude on a constant heading, ±10°, or 20° bank turns, ±10°, that will induce an imminent stall.
5. Applies proper control to maintain coordinated flight.
6. Recognizes and recovers from imminent stalls at the first indication of buffeting or decay of control effectiveness by reducing angle of attack and adjusting power, as necessary, to regain normal flight attitude.
7. Avoids full stall, secondary stall, excessive airspeed, excessive altitude change, spin, and flight below 1,500 feet AGL.

D. **TASK:** **MANEUVERING AT CRITICALLY SLOW AIRSPEED** (ASEL)

PILOT OPERATION – 4

REFERENCE: AC 61-21.

Objective. To determine that the applicant:

1. Exhibits knowledge by explaining the flight characteristics and controllability associated with maneuvering at critically slow airspeeds.
2. Selects an entry altitude that will allow the maneuver to be performed no lower than 1,500 feet AGL.
3. Establishes and maintains a critically slow airspeed while –

   (a) in coordinated straight and turning flight in various configurations and bank angles, and
   (b) in coordinated departure climbs and landing approach descents in various configurations.

4. Maintains the desired altitude, ±100 feet, when a

constant altitude is specified, and levels off from climbs and descents, ±100 feet.

5. Maintains the desired heading during straight flight, ±10°.
6. Maintains the specified bank angle, ±10°, in coordinated flight.
7. Maintains a critically slow airspeed, +5, -0 knots.

E.   TASK: CONSTANT ALTITUDE TURNS (ASEL)

PILOT OPERATION – 10

REFERENCE: AC 61-21.

Objective.   To determine that the applicant:

1. Exhibits knowledge by explaining the performance factors associated with constant altitude turns, including increased load factors, power required, and overbanking tendency.
2. Selects an altitude that will allow the maneuver to be performed no lower than 1,500 feet AGL.
3. Establishes an airspeed which does not exceed the airplane design maneuvering airspeed.
4. Enters a 360° turn maintaining a bank angle of 40° to 50° in coordinated flight.
5. Divides attention between airplane control and orientation.
6. Rolls out at the desired heading, ±10°.
7. Maintains the desired altitude, ±100 feet.

VIII.   AREA OF OPERATION:
FLIGHT MANEUVERING BY REFERENCE TO GROUND OBJECTS

NOTE: This AREA OF OPERATION is NOT required for the addition of a single–engine land class rating.

A.   TASK: RECTANGULAR COURSE (ASEL)

PILOT OPERATION – 3

REFERENCE: AC 61-21.

Objective.   To determine that the applicant:

1. Exhibits knowledge by explaining wind–drift correction in straight–and–turning flight, and the relationship of the rectangular course to airport traffic patterns.
2. Selects a suitable reference area.
3. Enters a left or right pattern at a desired distance from the selected reference area and at 600 to 1,000 feet AGL.
4. Divides attention between airplane control and ground track, and maintains coordinated flight.
5. Applies the necessary wind–drift corrections during straight–and–turning flight to maintain the desired ground track.
6. Maintains the desired altitude, ±100 feet.
7. Maintains the desired airspeed, ±10 knots.
8. Avoids bank angles in excess of 45°.
9. Reverses course, as directed by the examiner.

B.   TASK: S–TURNS ACROSS A ROAD (ASEL)

PILOT OPERATION – 3

REFERENCE: AC 61-21.

Objective.   To determine that the applicant:

1. Exhibits adequate knowledge by explaining the

procedures and wind–drift correction associated with S–turns.
2. Selects a suitable ground reference line.
3. Enters perpendicular to the selected reference line at 600 to 1,000 feet AGL.
4. Divides attention between airplane control and ground track, and maintains coordinated flight.
5. Applies the necessary wind–drift correction to track a constant radius turn on each side of the selected reference line.
6. Reverses the direction of turn directly over the selected reference line.
7. Maintains the desired altitude, ±100 feet.
8. Maintains the desired airspeed, ±10 knots.

C.   TASK: TURNS AROUND A POINT (ASEL)

PILOT OPERATION – 3

REFERENCE: AC 61-21.

Objective.   To determine that the applicant:

1. Exhibits knowledge by explaining the procedures and wind–drift correction associated with turns around a point.
2. Selects suitable ground reference points.
3. Enters a left or right turn at a desired distance from the selected reference point at 600 to 1,000 feet AGL.
4. Divides attention between airplane control and ground track, and maintains coordinated flight.
5. Applies the necessary wind–drift corrections to track a constant–radius turn around the selected reference point.
6. Maintains the desired altitude, ±100 feet.
7. Maintains the desired airspeed, ±10 knots.

IX.   AREA OF OPERATION:
NIGHT FLIGHT OPERATIONS

NOTE: This AREA OF OPERATION is NOT required for the addition of a single–engine land class rating. However, if the applicant is to be evaluated on night flying operations, then the examiner must evaluate elements 1 through 3. Elements 4 through 8 may be evaluated at the option of the examiner.

Night flight operations will be evaluated ONLY if the applicant meets night flying regulatory requirements. If this AREA OF OPERATION is not evaluated, the applicant's certificate will bear the limitation, "Night Flying Prohibited."

A.   TASK: NIGHT FLIGHT (ASEL)

PILOT OPERATION – 9

REFERENCES: AC 61-21, AC 67-2.

Objective.   To determine that the applicant:

1. Explains preparation, equipment, and factors essential to night flight.
2. Determines airplane, airport, and navigation lighting.
3. Exhibits knowledge by explaining night flying procedures, including safety precautions and emergency actions.
4. Inspects the airplane by following the checklist which includes items essential for night flight operations.
5. Starts, taxies, and performs pretakeoff check adhering to good operating practices.
6. Performs takeoffs and climbs with emphasis on visual references.
7. Navigates and maintains orientation under VFR conditions.

8. Approaches and lands adhering to good operating practices for night flight operations.

X. AREA OF OPERATION:
EMERGENCY OPERATIONS

A. TASK: EMERGENCY APPROACH AND LANDING (SIMULATED) (ASEL)

PILOT OPERATION – 10

REFERENCES: AC 61-21; Airplane Handbook and Flight Manual.

Objective. To determine that the applicant:

1. Exhibits knowledge by explaining approach and landing procedures to be used in various emergencies.
2. Establishes and maintains the recommended best–glide airspeed and configuration during simulated emergencies.
3. Selects a suitable landing area within gliding distance.
4. Plans and follows a flight pattern to the selected landing area, considering altitude, wind, terrain, obstructions, and other factors.
5. Follows an appropriate emergency checklist.
6. Attempts to determine the reason for the simulated malfunction.
7. Maintains positive control of the airplane.

NOTE: Examiner should terminate the emergency approach at or above minimum safe altitude.

B. TASK: SYSTEM AND EQUIPMENT MALFUNCTIONS (ASEL)

PILOT OPERATION – 10

REFERENCES: AC 61-21; Airplane Handbook and Flight Manual.

Objective. To determine that the applicant:

1. Exhibits knowledge by explaining causes of, indications of, and pilot actions for, malfunctions of various systems and equipment.
2. Analyzes the situation and takes appropriate action for simulated emergencies such as –

   (a) partial power loss.
   (b) rough running engine or overheat.
   (c) carburetor or induction icing.
   (d) loss of oil pressure.
   (e) fuel starvation.
   (f) engine compartment fire.
   (g) electrical system malfunction.
   (h) gear or flap malfunction.
   (i) door opening in flight.
   (j) trim inoperative.
   (k) loss of pressurization.
   (l) other malfunctions.

XI. AREA OF OPERATION:
APPROACHES AND LANDINGS

A. TASK: NORMAL AND CROSSWIND APPROACHES AND LANDINGS (ASEL)

PILOT OPERATION – 5

REFERENCES: AC 61-21; Airplane Handbook and Flight Manual.

Objective. To determine that the applicant:

1. Exhibits knowledge by explaining the elements of normal and crosswind approaches and landings, including airspeeds, configurations, crosswind limitations, and related safety factors.
2. Maintains the proper ground track on final approach.
3. Establishes the approach and landing configuration and power required.
4. Maintains the recommended approach airspeed, ±5 knots.
5. Makes smooth, timely, and correct control application during the final approach and transition from approach to landing roundout.
6. Touches down smoothly at approximate stalling speed, at or within 500 feet beyond a specified point, with no appreciable drift, and the airplane longitudinal axis aligned with the runway centerline.
7. Maintains directional control, increasing aileron deflection into the wind, as necessary, during the after–landing roll.

NOTE: If a crosswind condition does not exist, the applicant's knowledge of the TASK will be evaluated through oral testing.

B. TASK: FORWARD SLIPS TO LANDING (ASEL)

PILOT OPERATION – 5

REFERENCE: AC 61-21.

Objective. To determine that the applicant:

1. Exhibits knowledge by explaining the elements of a forward slip to a landing, including the purpose, technique, limitation, and the effect on airspeed indications.
2. Establishes a forward slip at a point from which a landing can be made in a desired area using the recommended airspeed and configuration.
3. Maintains a ground track aligned with the runway centerline.
4. Maintains an airspeed which results in minimum floating during the landing roundout.
5. Recovers smoothly from the slip.
6. Touches down smoothly at approximate stalling speed, at and within 500 feet beyond a specified point, with no appreciable drift, and the airplane longitudinal axis aligned with the runway centerline.
7. Maintains directional control during the after–landing roll.

C. TASK: GO–AROUND (ASEL)

PILOT OPERATION – 5

REFERENCES: AC 61-21; Airplane Handbook and Flight Manual.

Objective. To determine that the applicant:

1. Exhibits knowledge by explaining the elements of the go–around procedure, including proper decision, recommended airspeeds, drag effect of wing flaps and landing gear, and coping with undesirable pitch and yaw.
2. Makes a proper decision to go around.
3. Applies takeoff power and establishes the proper pitch attitude to attain the recommended airspeed.
4. Retracts the wing flaps, as recommended, and at a safe altitude.

5. Retracts the landing gear, if retractable, after a positive rate of climb has been established.
6. Trims the airplane and climbs at V_Y ±5 knots, and tracks the appropriate traffic pattern.

D. TASK: SHORT–FIELD APPROACH AND LANDING (ASEL)

PILOT OPERATION – 8

REFERENCES: AC 61-21; Airplane Handbook and Flight Manual.

Objective. To determine that the applicant:

1. Exhibits knowledge by explaining the elements of a short–field approach and landing, including airspeed, configuration, and related safety factors.
2. Considers obstructions, landing surface, and wind conditions.
3. Selects a suitable touchdown point.
4. Establishes the short–field approach and landing configuration, airspeed, and descent angle.
5. Maintains control of the descent rate and the recommended airspeed, ±5 knots, along the extended runway centerline.
6. Touches down at or within 200 feet beyond a specified point, with minimum float, no appreciable drift, and the airplane longitudinal axis aligned with the runway centerline.
7. Maintains directional control during the after–landing roll.

8. Applies braking and controls, as necessary, to stop in the shortest distance consistent with safety.

E. TASK: SOFT–FIELD APPROACH AND LANDING (ASEL)

PILOT OPERATION – 8

REFERENCES: AC 61-21; Airplane Handbook and Flight Manual.

Objective. To determine that the applicant:

1. Exhibits knowledge by explaining the elements of a soft–field approach and landing procedure, including airspeeds, configurations, operations on various surfaces, and related safety factors.
2. Evaluates obstructions, landing surface, and wind conditions.
3. Establishes the recommended soft–field approach and landing configuration and airspeed.
4. Maintains recommended airspeed, ±5 knots, along the extended runway centerline.
5. Touches down smoothly at minimum descent rate and groundspeed, with no appreciable drift, and the airplane longitudinal axis aligned with runway centerline.
6. Maintains directional control during the after–landing roll.
7. Maintains proper position of flight controls and sufficient speed to taxi on soft surface.

Index

Index

Index

Edited by Carl H. Silverman

Other Bestsellers From TAB

☐ **THE LADY BE GOOD: MYSTERY BOMBER OF WORLD WAR II**—Dennis E. McClendon

What happened to the B-24 bomber nicknamed "The Lady Be Good," and its nine young American crewmembers when they vanished without a trace in 1943? An exhaustive post-war search produced no clues. Then—16 years later—the B-24 was found deep in the Sahara desert. Step-by-step the author pieces together the solution to the bomber's fate. 208 pp., illustrated.

Paper $10.95   **Hard $12.95**
Book No. 26624

☐ **FROM WHITE KNUCKLES TO COCKPIT COOL**—Ava and David Carmichael

Here's an indispensable, basic guide to general aviation written for those having their first experience with light aircraft. Everyone will enjoy this lighthearted look at the thoughts and fears of those reluctant to fly. It is for anyone who logs a lot of flying time sitting nervously beside the pilot. Illustrated with cartoons, photos, charts and check lists, this book is a must for the apprehensive "backseat pilot." 144 pp.

Paper $8.95   **Hard $9.95**
Book No. 25850

☐ **GUADALCANAL—THE ISLAND OF FIRE: REFLECTIONS OF THE 347TH FIGHTER GROUP**—Robert Lawrence Ferguson

A first-hand account of the Battle of Guadalcanal from a member of the famed "Game Cock Squadron." August 7, 1987 marked the 45th anniversary of one of the hardest fought battles in history. This gripping on-the-scene report captures not only the almost constant action, but the impossible conditions under which the beleaguered Americans withstood a larger and better equipped Japanese army. 272 pp., 74 illus.

Paper $13.95   **Hard $16.95**
Book No. 22389

☐ **FLYING AS IT WAS . . . TRUE STORIES FROM AVIATION'S PAST**—Gerry A. Casey

Every aviation enthusiast who has ever enjoyed Gerry Casey's popular columns in *Private Pilot* or *Pacific Flyer* magazines knows that here is a writer who really knows how to spin a fascinating tale! Now, for the first time, the very best of Casey's *Flying As It Was* column from *Private Pilot*, along with some of his best stories published by *Pacific Flyer*, have been collected into a single volume that's guaranteed to provide you with hours of entertaining reading! 256 pp., 30 illus.

Paper $11.95   **Hard $14.95**
Book No. 2403

☐ **HOWARD HUGHES AND HIS FLYING BOAT**—Charles Barton

The real story of Howard Hughes—aviator, innovative inventor and designer—has never before been told. But in this award-winning book, for the first time, large numbers of former Hughes employees and close associates talk about their famous boss. In addition to the first-hand reminiscences of many who knew and worked for Howard Hughes this book is based on previously unpublished material. 272 pp., Illustrated Throughout.

Paper $13.95   **Hard $15.95**
Book No. 26456

☐ **AIM/FAR 1988**—The TAB/AERO Staff

New Federal Aviation Administration (FAA) regulations included in the 1988 edition of this essential sourcebook for pilots are: Part 43—Maintenance, Preventive Maintenance, Rebuilding and Alteration; Part 73—Special Use Airspace; Part 105—Parachute Jumping; Part 141—Pilot Schools; and, Part 143—Ground Instructors. Also contains complete FAA basic flight information, ATC procedures, and "A.M. Weather" broadcast schedule. 416 pp., illustrated

Paper $13.95   **Hard $18.95**
Book No. 24388

☐ **WINGS OF THE WEIRD AND WONDERFUL**—Captain Eric Brown

The Guinness Book of Records lists Captain Eric "Winkle" Brown, the former Chief Naval Test Pilot and Commanding Officer of Great Britain's Aerodynamic Flight at the Royal Aircraft Establishment, as having flown more types of aircraft than any other pilot in the world! Though his test and naval flying writings are already internationally known, he has once more opened his flying logbooks to reveal some of the more unusual types of aircraft. 176 pp., 77 illus.

Paper $15.95   **Hard $19.95**
Book No. 2404

☐ **THE ILLUSTRATED HANDBOOK OF AVIATION AND AEROSPACE FACTS**—Joe Christy

A complete look at American aviation—civil and military. All the political, social, economic, and personality factors that have influenced the state of U.S. military airpower, the boom-and-bust cycles in Civil aviation, America's manned and unmanned space flights, and little-known facts on the flights, and little-known facts on the birth of modern rocketry, it's all here in this complete sourcebook! 480 pp., 486 illus.

Paper $24.95   **Hard $29.50**
Book No. 2397

Other Bestsellers From TAB